CW01501892

First English edition published in 2

The moral right of Jason J Smart to be identified as the author of this
work had been asserted in accordance with the Copyright, Designs
and Patents Act, 1988

Cover design by Ace Graphics

ASIN: B01KQNALKE
ISBN-13: 978-1534730793
ISBN-10:1534730796

Smart, Jason J
Africa to Asia

Africa to Asia

One man, two continents, eleven countries

Jason Smart

Contents:

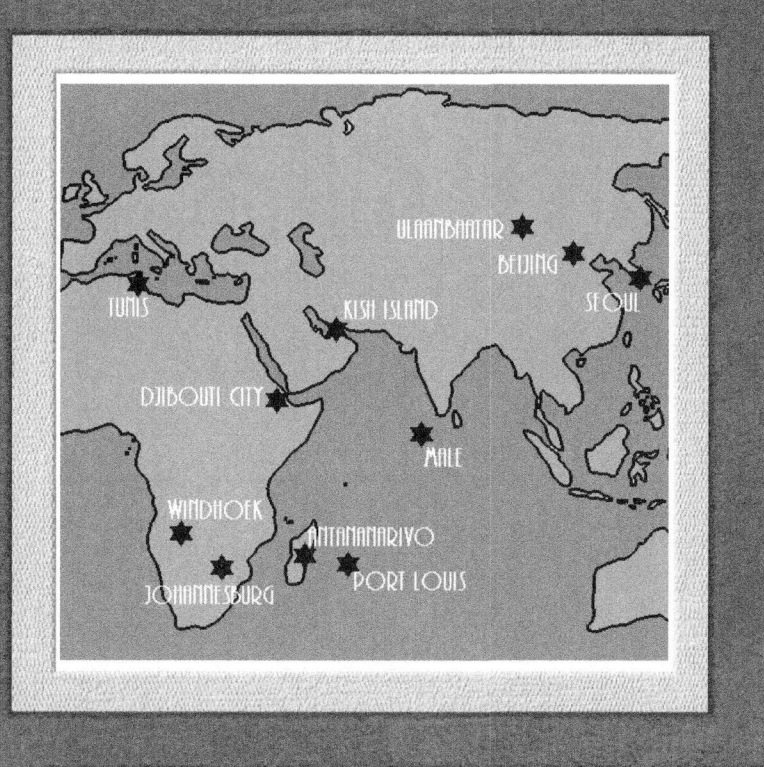

For Ray and Joyce, fellow travellers, even in their Autumnal years

Part 1

Africa

Djibouti, Mauritius, Madagascar, Namibia, South Africa, Tunisia

Chapter 1: Djibouti City: the City of Dust and Litter

The immigration officer at Djibouti-Ambouli International Airport looked bored out of his mind. He was in no rush to sort out my visa. While a hot African sun blazed outside and sweat dribbled inside, he waved me over to a cheap plastic chair in the corner of the stuffy terminal. I was the only passenger remaining from my inbound flight. When the man yawned and looked down at his phone, I walked towards the seat.

Five minutes later, another immigration officer appeared. "You are seaman?" he asked.

It seemed an unusual question, unless he meant it as an insult. Or perhaps he had seen my entrance into the terminal. Whenever I arrive in a new country, I celebrate with a carefully choreographed 1940s sailor routine, complete with cheesy grin, tap dancing and slapping of thighs.

"No, I'm not in the navy."

"Army?"

I shook my head and the man asked to see my passport. I stood and handed it over. He opened it at the personal information page. "Canadian?"

"British." I pointed to where it stated my nationality.

"British? Why you come Djibouti?"

"Tourist."

The thin man didn't say anything and then walked off with my passport. I sat down, wondering whether I would ever get into Djibouti. It was supposed to be an easy process, or so I had been told. Slumping into the curve of the seat, I was surprised when a third man arrived. This one was older and had a few epaulets on his shoulder. He studied me, studied my passport and then asked where I was staying. I told him the Sheraton.

"Where go after Djibouti?"

"Nairobi. In two days."

"You have airline ticket for Nairobi?"

I showed him. This seemed to do the trick. He nodded and took me into a tiny side room I had not noticed before. A man was sitting at a desk covered in paper and random stationery. He was leaning back in a chair, half asleep. After both men conferred for a moment, the formerly slouching man wrote something in a ledger, asked for sixty dollars and then issued me with a three-day Djiboutian visa. It had only taken an hour and a half.

2

A few hours previously, I had been sitting inside a Kenyan Airways jet bound for Djibouti City. Nine of my fellow passengers were Chinese businessmen; six more were Africans, leaving me as the sixteenth passenger. Quite clearly, Djibouti was not a hot destination.

An hour after take-off, we began our descent. Below us, the beginnings of human settlement began to replace the sharp, weathered ridges that had crisscrossed the endless East African dustbowl. As we flew lower, the city limits appeared beneath the wings: a low-rise collection of haphazard, simple dwellings interspersed with the occasional mosque. A layer of brown-orange dust covered everything. It was as if a giant bag of sand had burst in the sky above Djibouti City, coating everything and anything.

We landed soon after. One side of Djibouti-Ambouli International Airport was for civilian aircraft, the other for military. As we turned off the runway, I gazed out at a neat row of grey Hercules transport planes. They belonged to American forces. Before I could study them further, we were heading for the passenger terminal. It was time to get my Djiboutian visa on arrival.

3

Djibouti should be a Red Sea paradise, yet it is not. It should be attracting high-end holidaymakers to laze around on its palm-fringed beaches, but they do not come. And the reason is simple: Djibouti does not need them.

Most people have never heard of Djibouti. But those who have know that the tiny country (Djibouti is not much larger than Wales) is sandwiched between the tourist hotspots of Somalia, Yemen and Eritrea. In fact, the Somali border is only twenty kilometres from Djibouti City. Yemen is only a short boat ride across the Red Sea, and is so close that on clear days it is sometimes visible on the horizon. Eritrea, a country described as Africa's North Korea, spans Djibouti's northern border. Yet, despite these neighbours from hell, Djibouti is one of the safest countries in Africa.

There are thousands of reasons: each one an American, Japanese, French, German or Spanish military man or woman. Djibouti lies along one of the most strategically important shipping routes of the Red Sea. The Port of Djibouti is one the busiest in the region, and is therefore a good vantage point to protect the busy shipping lanes of the Suez Canal from Somali pirates. And, with access to the Middle East literally around the corner, foreign troops can conduct drone attacks in Yemen, Somalia and as far away as Afghanistan. So, with countless foreign dollars literally flying into Djibouti, you can see why they are not bothered about tourism.

Outside the airport, a hawker tried to pick up my bag. I waved him off, telling him I did not need any assistance. When he tried again, I told him, "*No!*" He got the message and returned to his station by the door, looking sullen. With arriving passengers so thin on the ground, it was no wonder. But, with only a single piece of hand luggage, I was perfectly capable of wheeling it myself.

I was following an employee of the Sheraton Djibouti Hotel. The sun was high in the African sky, a blaze of yellow that had me reaching for my sunglasses. It was hot, too. April marked the onset of the hot season where temperatures spiked to over 40 degrees Celsius. While the driver made a phone call, I stood in the heat. I didn't mind, for it gave me a chance to take stock. Djibouti looked dry and dusty; even the trees looked in need of water, their leaves crispy and parched. Rough sand and scorched soil made up the view on the side of the road, with a bleached single-storey building straight in front. While I was thinking that the airport would not win any awards for its looks, the driver finished his conversation and gestured I should climb into the back of his minivan.

Beyond the airport perimeter, we traversed the streets of Djibouti City, passing broken pavements that led to cracked walls and decrepit buildings. The only people I could see were blank-faced men, either traipsing along the edge of the road or lurking in doorways. Further on, we drove by a row of fancier-looking dwellings, all protected by spiked fences and barbed wire. Each home featured wide verandas, Arabian-style arches and satellite dishes: homes of the rich, I thought. Soon we arrived at a coastal road, pleasingly named Rue de la Siesta. On my right was the Red Sea, a hazy expanse of blue bordered by a strip of bare sand. Nobody sunbathed in Djibouti, at least not at midday.

The Sheraton Djibouti is located at the eastern tip of Djibouti City, on a spindly peninsular flanked by the Red Sea. It is the second-best hotel in the country, about half the price of the best: the Kempinski Palace. As the Red Sea fell away, we were back to the grime of the city: litter piled against tree trunks, men sitting around doing nothing in particular and old green and white taxis parked anywhere and everywhere.

A haphazard group of armed soldiers and policemen blocked the road to the Sheraton, protecting it from insurgent attack. They were waiting near an armoured vehicle, lazing around on cheap chairs under the shade of a large tree. Since I was in the Sheraton's own shuttle bus, they simply waved us through. At the end of the thin road was the hotel, but before we got there, we stopped again: a small security hut was in operation. While a man checked the underside of the minivan for explosives, I walked through an airport-style metal detector. Through the other side, I spied a military ambulance. It was as if I had arrived into an army camp.

The hotel was palatial, featuring a pool, tropical palm trees and an expanse of blue water. There were a few Western sunbathers together with a smattering of Chinese businessmen. The former were out by the pool, the latter were sitting in the lobby staring at laptops. A large poster told me a live band would be playing in the bar later that evening.

A soldier walked past me. Then another and then one more. Beige uniforms were everywhere, all of them belonging to German troops. Later, I found out they were permanent guests of the hotel. I checked in and threw my things in the room. From the window, I gazed down at the tiny beach. Two Western children were playing on it, close to a woman on a sun lounger. It was likely that she was in Djibouti visiting her army husband, I thought. Beyond the trio was the sea. If I ignored the ramshackle buildings at the other side of the bay, I might have been in Dubai or Sharm el Sheik. Maybe.

I decided to investigate the pool area. Donning my cheap, knock-off Ray-Bans, I headed outside. With the well-placed palm trees, the hotel looked *exotic*; a world away from the real city. And I looked the part too: a western man in cool shades. *Cheap* cool shades.

A couple of soldiers came out of a small mustard-coloured building ahead of me. In a moment of terrible coincidence, they passed at the exact moment my sunglasses decided to fall apart. A dark piece of cheap plastic slipped from one rim and fell to the ground. No warning, no delay: one second it was covering my eye, the next it was gone. Even the clatter sounded cheap. All three of us looked at the piece of fallen plastic and then the men were gone. I scooped the lens up, removed my glasses and threw everything in the bin. This was a great start to my trip around Africa. Day one and my sunglasses were in bits.

I decided the pool held no interest for me and entered the lobby to find the exit. It was time to leave the plush hotel and see the real Djibouti City. Once outside, I squinted in the sun, ambling by the ambulance, the metal detector hut and the military checkpoint. At the other side of the gauntlet, I found myself near a roundabout called Place Tokyo. Why it was named after the Japanese capital, I had no idea, for it looked about as Japanese as I did. I stopped to see the lie of the land before me. It did not look inviting.

5

Litter was everywhere, as if a dumper truck had simply spewed its contents into the street. Random men were lazing about in whatever shade they could find – inside doorways, under trees, besides walls – all of them chewing *khat*, the ubiquitous drug of choice for men along the horn of Africa. For thousands of years, from the wilds of Yemen to the northern reaches of Kenya, millions of East African men (and sometimes women) had been chewing away on lumps of green leaves to get their stimulation. From what I could see, the men of Djibouti loved it, for all were munching away on the government-approved euphoria, cheeks bulging, teeth stained green. Every morning, fresh lorry loads arrived from neighbouring Ethiopia, which was then distributed among local khat sellers, who sold it to their customers. I read that even though Khat is illegal in much of the world, certain governments along the Horn of Africa allow its use because it keeps young and potentially angry men docile. If that was the reason, then it was working a treat, at least judging by the slumbering and mainly horizontal men near Place Tokyo. None of them looked capable of staging a game of cards, let alone a riot.

Apart from the litter and people, the third thing that struck me was the quality of the buildings. Many seemed decayed, caked in a disgusting layer of black from the traffic fumes, crumbling upon the foundations from which they were built. A shout made me turn around. It was a taxi driver. His vehicle had stopped just behind me. I waved him away and headed towards the centre along Boulevard de la Republique, Djibouti City's main thoroughfare.

Cracked pavements, barbed wire coils sitting atop walls and more men chewing khat met my every move. I finally spied a woman covered in a swirl of bright fabric. She disappeared into a dusty doorway. In front of me, perhaps fifty metres away, was a policeman. He was carrying a lunchbox. I pondered whether it was from a crime scene until I saw him veer off towards a khat stand where he filled it with green shrubbery. The vehicles passing me were taxis, falling-to-bits trucks or fume-belching minibuses. And despite the proximity to the sea, squat black crows were the bird of choice in Djibouti. A trio of them were perched in a tree in front of me. One had a long bread roll in its beak. Behind it, a plastic bag fluttered in the breeze like a broken flag. The bird took a bite and then the bread fell to the pavement. The crow issued a squawk of consternation and then flew to retrieve it.

Further along was a cinema, its tall white tower spelling out ODEON in large red letters. The tower jutted upwards, as if trying to escape the white monstrosity that formed its base. It looked like a bomb had detonated inside the cinema, though a more probable explanation was simple abandonment. That was it, I realised. Djibouti City was a neglected place, a city where repairs were not on the agenda and its citizens did not care

Around the corner, something made me stop in my tracks. A man herding seven goats was about to run past me, his animals trotting happily in the road even though a series of battered taxis were just inches away from their feet. The man was carrying a long stick and, as he and his beastly squad approached, I took cover in a dusty alcove near a line of khat sellers. As the goats trotted by, I studied the khat vendors. There were three of them, with the most salubrious establishment housed inside an actual shop, the seller's wares proudly laid over the counter. The other two were simply street peddlers sitting in the dust with tied bunches of green leaves in front of them on a cloth. When a man noticed me and held up a bag of green leaves, I left the alcove and walked on.

"Ça va?" called the black-toothed man sitting outside a tiny convenience store. Above it was a concrete hellhole that called itself the Bank of Africa. He was stick thin, gaunt faced and had the tell-tale signs of a seasoned khat chewer: disgusting blackened green stains on his teeth.

"Ça va, très bien," I replied: the standard greeting I would give over the next few hours. Being the only white face, I was attracting many glances, though none were hostile. Djibouti had once been a French colony and the language lived on among the local Djiboutian population. Many of the street names had a link to the old country, too: Boulevard du General de Gaulle, Rue de Marseille and Rue de Paris being just a few. The man looked at me, but I did not linger, for I had spied a striking white and turquoise minaret poking from behind some nondescript buildings.

I found myself underneath the striking Sada Mosque, its minaret offering a glimpse of beauty amid the grime and dust at street level. Its main section was nowhere near as nice as its tower and so, with the sudden arrival of another khat chewer, this one upwardly mobile and wanting to offer his services as a guide, I moved on.

It was so damned hot. Without my sunglasses, my eyes were stinging, especially with the sweat pouring down my face and so, to escape the relentless sun, I found a bar. It was dimly lit, but its stock of Ethiopian beer was ice cold. I took my bottle to an empty seat near the window. A few tables away sat a couple of middle-aged Western men drinking coffee. I nodded at them, hoping they would be amenable for a chat but when neither seemed inclined, I looked outside. The view was of ruined buildings and dusty side streets.

The two men were joined by a third. "Thank Christ, I'm outta here tomorrow," the newcomer said in an American accent. "Total shithole."

His companions nodded, one of them adding, "An overpriced shithole."

I could concur with that. My small bottle had cost me 900 Djiboutian francs, which was five dollars. A sandwich at the hotel had set me back almost twenty. Djibouti was easily the most expensive country I'd visited in Africa. Thank God I was only here for two days. Tuning the men's conversation out, which mainly concerned the state of the city's roads, I discovered the bar had some free Wi-Fi. I decided to go on the British Foreign Office website to see what it said about Djibouti. '*A suicide bombing at La Chaumiere restaurant in Djibouti city on 24 May 2014 resulted in a number of fatalities and serious casualties, including western nationals. Exercise extreme vigilance in public places frequented by foreigners.*'

Shit on a stick! I was sitting in that very restaurant! A quick Google search revealed more. On a busy Saturday night, almost two years previously, La Chaumiere's bar was busy with Westerners, mostly military personnel enjoying a night out. At some point, with the beer flowing nicely, a Somali man and his female friend entered the bar and sat down. No one gave the pair a second glance, but if they had, they might have noticed their bulky clothing. But it would have been too late: the couple, Somali militants belonging to al-Shabaab, an affiliate of Al-Qaeda, had already detonated their suicide vests. In the resulting carnage, eleven soldiers were injured and three people killed, including the murderous couple.

I looked about me, searching out anyone who might be watching me a little too closely, but all I could see were a few groups of Western men. I reckoned they were all soldiers. I drained the last of my beer and headed outside.

7

More grime and filth coated the hectic marketplace. Dusty alleyways led off in all directions from it. Garbage filled every crack in the pavement and sealed every hole in the road. A man wandered by and dropped an empty can on the ground. It was one of hundreds.

Around the edge, men sat doing nothing. I wandered through some of the stalls, finding that most were purveyors of either khat or tat, which I thought was a good name for a shop in Djibouti. In the latter category were kitchen utensils, supposedly from France, black abayas from Dubai and delicious bananas from Djibouti. Khat stalls outnumbered them all. At the other end of the market, I found myself at the edge of a square called Place Mahmoud Harbi, named after a 1950s politician who had once sent a lion to the King of Saudi Arabia as a gift. Instead of grand buildings, statues and waterfalls, the square was a horrendous melting pot of faded colonial buildings, honking minibuses, loitering green taxis and bunches of people doing nothing in particular – in other words, a typical down-at-heel African quarter. I stopped to take a photo.

"Hey!" yelled a voice. It was a khat seller: a young man sitting under the shade offered by a huge *Dove Cream* billboard. For softer, smoother and glowing skin, it stated. "No photo!"

I took a photo anyway and then lowered my camera. This man hadn't been the first local to warn me about taking snaps. A snaggle-toothed man had told me off for taking a photo of the mosque I'd seen earlier and, just a few minutes after that, another man had followed me up a street admonishing me for taking a snap of a goat. I moved on, angry with people wanting to thwart me taking photographs. The only other country I'd been to as bad for this was Turkmenistan. But there, the camera naysayers had been soldiers guarding their photogenic statues and buildings. Here, it was the locals barring me from taking photos of dirty streets and grimy bus stations.

I headed south and found another herd of goats blocking my path. About fifteen of them were galloping toward me, one running with such abandon that I could see its elongated udders swinging perilously. As it passed, I realised it only had two udders, which meant they were not udders, but testicles. As I considered this, the rest of the goats raced past me. Five seconds later, a harried man sprinted after them, clicking and whirring his tongue. I carried on with my sightseeing, in this most ugly of African cities.

8

I came across a small supermarket: boarded-up windows, heavy duty bars across the door, and then a series of threadbare shelves inside, with a couple of chains snaking across the floor for no fathomable reason except to trip shoppers up, made me think of a prison. Except I knew the prisons in Djibouti were much worse. Stifling temperatures, cruel guards and tiny cramped cells were just some of the amenities on offer, at least according to the British Foreign Office website. Sanitary conditions would be 'poor' and the whole ambience 'harsh'. On the bright side, I would receive three meals a day with 'meat served on alternate days'.

I left the supermarket after buying a large bottle of water. The first thing I did with it was wash my grime-caked hands. A little girl watched me do this and then rushed over with her hand outstretched: the first beggar I'd come across in the country. I brushed her away, not wanting to be surrounded by others, and she gave up after only a few metres. I then began a long trek back northwards, leaving behind the madness of downtown until I found myself walking along a narrow stretch of road known as the causeway. It bisected a small sheltered part of the Red Sea. The traffic was light, made up of the occasional wheezing truck and a man on a cart pulled along by a donkey. In the water to my right, a couple of young men were standing thigh-deep in the water, holding a homemade net between them. I watched as they dragged it towards the rocky shore, and then saw their disappointment when they raised it up to reveal only a single crab.

Abandoning the French theme for once, the city planners of Djibouti City had named the causeway the Route de Venice, though the only link I could see with the Italian city was the water. With the late afternoon sun still beating down on my head, I passed two wooden dhows. Both were badly damaged, abandoned on a muddy sandbank. Behind them sat a giant red container ship. Armies of stork-like cranes were unloading it and similarly-sized vessels. The area I was looking at was Port de Djibouti: the lifeblood of the city and off-limits to tourists.

Instead, I continued with my walk along the causeway, coming within sight of the Presidential Palace. It was an expansive white complex full of arches and palatial curves, surrounded by gardens dotted with exotic trees and exciting fauna. It was easily the nicest part of Djibouti City, but one I would not be able to see up close. For one thing, the palace was set back some distance from the road, protected by a heavily-guarded perimeter wall; for another, a guard was watching me. I snapped off a sneaky photo, waited for a gunshot, but, when it did not materialise, scurried away, turning off the causeway at its northern end.

Half an hour later, I was back at the Sheraton. I was weary, caked in dust, but pleased I had taken some time to see the city up close. Tomorrow promised more fun, though, because I would be driving to the lowest point in the whole of the African continent. But, for now, all I wanted was a shower and a cold beer. I had survived my first full day in Africa.

Clockwise from top left: The Sheraton Djibouti – nice beach and pool area, but full of soldiers; The Odeon cinema has seen better days; Place Mahmoud Harbi, in the heart of the old town; Abandoned dhows with Djibouti Port in the background; The president of Djibouti; The striking minaret belonging to the Sada Mosque

Chapter 2: Road trip to the lowest point in Africa

I was up early for my 7am tour to Lake Assal. Outside my window, the sun loungers were empty and the only person I could see was a man with a brush. The sun was shining, though, casting slivers of translucent white across the rolling waves.

I went downstairs for something to eat, finding the breakfast restaurant full of soldiers. It was as if I was in a military mess hall. I grabbed a croissant and downed a cup of coffee. Then I sneezed. I could feel the beginnings of a cold.

I met Omar, my guide for the day. He was waiting in the lobby for me. Omar was a lean, thin faced man in his late twenties who could speak five languages (French, English, Arabic, Afar and Somali). "So let's go to the car," he said. "We have a three-hour drive ahead."

The car was a battered Toyota Hilux parked next to a Land Cruiser. The latter probably belonged to one of the German officers staying at the Sheraton. I climbed into the back of the Hilux, and Omar introduced me to the driver, Abdur, a man in his forties, as lean as Omar, but with the deeply-stained front teeth of a seasoned khat chewer.

"Okay," said Omar, "We will leave the city via the causeway. Then we will head west, passing through the Djiboutian countryside. Along the way, we will stop for breakfast. Does this sound favourable to you?"

I nodded assent and, when the engine rumbled into life, I sat back, looking forward to my trip to Lake Assal. As well as being the lowest point in Africa, the salt lake was surrounded by huge fields of volcanic rock. Visiting them was also part of the tour. The day promised plenty.

Due to the early hour, the streets of Djibouti City were mostly clear of traffic, which meant we could move quickly. But just as we were gathering speed, Abdur pulled in near a row of shacks. Omar jumped out and returned a few minutes later with a few packages wrapped in foil. "Breakfast, Jason," he said. "Haricot beans." He unwrapped one package to reveal a serving of sloppy beans in red sauce. From another bag, he produced some bread rolls. He passed the beans and bread over and I ate my second Djiboutian breakfast of the day. Then he and Abdur ate theirs.

The causeway was the same as yesterday, with the red container ship still sitting in the port. At the other end, khat sellers were readying their wares, preparing for the morning rush, while goats milled about along dusty verges. Always dust, I had discovered. Djibouti City: the city of dust.

We negotiated a roundabout where a large face smiled at us. It was the Djiboutian president, Ismail Omar Guelle. He looked distinguished and wise. I asked Omar what the billboard was for.

"Elections. They are happening very soon."

"Do you think he will win?"

"I know he will."

The grimy shack-ridden outskirts finally fell behind, replaced by an arid landscape of stunted shrubs, blackened rubble and endless dirt. In the hazy distance were a few brown hills, some of them dotted with camels. The road that ran through the hinterlands was of good quality but too narrow for traffic using it. Trucks with Ethiopian plates plied both sides of the two-lane highway, either delivering supplies to the Djiboutian capital or returning to the border, a five-hour drive away. Whenever the gradient increased, the trucks slowed to a snail's pace. With no room to overtake, Abdur had no choice but to slow down too and light another of his seemingly endless supply of Benson & Hedges.

2

As half an hour turned into an hour, we began to pass small settlements made up of rounded shacks, herds of goats and camels and, occasionally, one or two discarded car tyres. Children tended the animals or carried bundles of sticks, toiling just as hard as the adults. Omar told me they were the Afar people, nomads who had crisscrossed Djibouti, Ethiopia and Eritrea for centuries. To build their shelters, they twisted tree branches into dome shapes and covered them with woven mats of palm leaves. "The Afar are free to move wherever they like. They do not need passports. If they want, they can move to Somalia and no one will stop them."

Something occurred to me. "How do the authorities know they are genuine nomads?"

Omar smiled. "Think about it. Nomads do not use official border crossings. They do not stroll up to the border with all the trucks and all the people and wait in line with their passports. No, they cross in the middle of the desert where there are no soldiers or any barriers. What normal person would do this? And another thing about nomads is their camels. How many people have you seen crossing a border with a herd of six or seven camels?"

"None."

"Exactly. Anyone with a herd of camels must be a nomad. They can move wherever they like."

I nodded at the logic, but thought it open to abuse. For a price, I could buy myself a herd of benevolent camels, wrap myself in authentic nomadic clothing, and then smuggle my way across the border with my cache of weapons. More likely, I could buy cheap goods in Ethiopia and then smuggle them back into Djibouti to sell at a massive profit. Which is, I later learned, exactly what happens.

Along my right-hand side were a series of black pipes laid out beside the highway's sandy edge. We had already passed hundreds of them, and hundreds more continued along the route, meandering along, up and down the contour of the land. I pointed them out to Omar.

"Water pipes," he said. "The Chinese put them there and will eventually dig them into the ground so they connect Ethiopia to Djibouti. Water will come down from the Ethiopian mountains, travelling over one hundred kilometres."

"Why are the Chinese doing it?" I wondered whether any of the men on my flight from Addis were working on it.

Omar shrugged. "The Chinese are everywhere in my country. They are building hospitals, making new roads and I think they are constructing a new railway line. There are even some Chinese restaurants in the city now."

Quite suddenly, a camel appeared in the road. Like a stunt driver, Abdur swerved away, saving the errant beast, and the car, from certain doom. In the rear window, I saw the camel nonchalantly sauntering over to the other side of the road towards a tree. A lorry blasted its horn to make it move. I turned to the front: Omar was tucking into his haricot beans while Abdur puffed on another Benson & Hedges. A camels running into the road, it appeared, was a frequent occurrence for them both.

3

An hour and ten minutes after leaving Djibouti City, we arrived at the town of Oueah (pronounced We-ah). Situated in the middle of a large dry valley, Oueah was a chaotic settlement that had grown around a large bend in the road. Its name was supremely apt because it meant 'turn' in the local language.

Since it was the first big town of note on the journey, it was a rest stop for trucks heading back to Ethiopia. As we slowed down, my eyes fixed upon the local restaurant. It was a tin-roofed wooden shack containing a single plastic table and three white plastic chairs. All of them were taken. Along from it, stalls were selling fruit, khat and assorted groceries while goats milled about with scrawny chickens. In one alcove, a woman wrapped in a purple and yellow shawl was selling packets of biscuits from a small metal dish.

Abdur pulled over and immediately a group of teenage boys huddled around his window. None seemed particularly surprised to see a white man in the back and instead were more interested in Omar. After shaking their hands, Omar said a few words to them.

They ran off and returned a minute later with handfuls of apples and thin cones of something wrapped in paper. Omar handed over some coins and passed me an apple and one of the cones. "Peanuts," he said.

The journey continued westwards until we came to a fork in the road. Ahead of us was Ethiopia: to our right, the lake. Before we turned, we stopped again. Any intersection in Djibouti meant a selling opportunity and this one was no different. Sellers of fruit (mainly apples and bananas), a shoe shiner, a hut selling convenience goods, and, of course, a khat vendor, were all in attendance. Abdur jumped out and headed straight for the khat. He returned with two bunches of the stuff. Omar asked whether I wanted to try some. I declined.

After a moment, Omar turned around. "Look, if you are not happy with us having khat in the car, then we will hide it and you will never see it again. You are in charge and we will do as you say."

I told him I was not bothered in the slightest about them having khat, and was actually quite interested in looking at it. Omar passed me a bunch. If I hadn't known otherwise, I would have assumed it was a bunch of basil. I sniffed a leaf. It smelled like basil, too. "How many leaves would I need to feel the effects?" I asked.

"Many of them. Enough to fill one side of your mouth."

I pulled off a single leaf to sample the taste. It tasted leafy, bitter and not very nice. Omar and Abdur laughed when I grimaced. I said, "Is it okay to drive under the influence of khat?" I'd read that some road accidents had been attributed to drivers using khat.

"Look," said Omar, "khat is okay unless a person is very tired. That is when the problems start. Take the truck drivers you have seen today. Many will travel one way, and then the other, all in a single day. To keep themselves alert, they will chew khat, and keep chewing it through the night. But their bodies and brains are tired. They are the ones who crash."

It seemed a valid point, and Abdur didn't look tired in the slightest. In fact, he was lighting another cigarette. "So how much did this bunch cost?"

"For one bunch it is five hundred franc, about three dollar."

With my blessing, Abdur wasted no time in pulling about fifteen leaves from his spindly bunch before stuffing them into his mouth. Then he mashed them together, sucking the water out and then crammed a whole load more in. One side of his face bulged like a hamster. With that, the engine rumbled back to life and we took the right-hand fork in the road.

4

The landscape was looking more volcanic. Large, angular rocks strewn across the darkening ground made the land look brooding. The only plants that could survive such an inhospitable environment were Acacia trees, their withered trunks and wide-spanning foliage dotting the otherwise desolate landscape. Then a row of other shrubs appeared, thinner than the acacias, but more abundant, at least in this region.

"They are devil trees," Omar said. "If an animal eats the leaves, it will die. If a person drinks milk from an infected animal, he will die too."

I wondered what sort of creatures could live outside but before I could ask, quite suddenly, Abdur wouldn't shut up. Speaking ten to the dozen in a language I could not understand, he and Omar began a protracted, mainly one-sided conversation. The khat was clearly working its magic. Then, mid-sentence Abdur stopped the car. Wondering what was going on, I watched as he reversed along the highway. When we stopped, he pointed outside. Standing maybe twenty feet away was a gazelle. The small, brown and white antelope was standing near an acacia tree, staring at the car, its huge elongated ears facing forward. After a second, it scampered off, nimbly negotiating the sharp volcanic rock. I looked at Abdur with renewed respect. Chewing khat had given him superhuman vision.

Later, we passed a small police station along a lonely stretch of road. Omar told me that, a few months previously, someone had murdered two policemen there. "We do not know the full details. All we know is that some men with guns stormed into the station and shot them. People say they were from Eritrea, which makes sense to me. They are jealous of us. They want to cause problems."

"Why?"

"They see that we are doing well – lots of foreign investment and army training – and they look at themselves. Their economy is going bad and their people are not happy. If I were them, I would not like this and be jealous. Also, Eritrea is paranoid we will invade their country with Ethiopia's help. They really hate the Ethiopians."

"How far is the Eritrean border from here?"

"Maybe one hundred and twenty kilometres – a two hour drive."

Soon, though, with the police station receding into the distance, we started driving through a wide volcanic region called the Afar Triple Junction. Cracks in the earth's surface ran through the ground like stitches in skin. Below the surface lay vast seas of magma, waiting to erupt, spewing poisonous sulphur and red-hot rock upon the land. Earthquakes were common in the Afar Triple Junction, Omar told me, as were volcanoes. "It is part of the great Africa Rift Valley, where three tectonic plates are trying to pull apart from each another. Every year, the Arabian plate pulls away from the African plate by eight millimetres. Eventually, this split will form a new sea and Africa's horn will be no more."

The road took a gradual downward gradient. Along both sides, tall hills grew, which turned to mountains at the horizon. Instead of dust, the land was windswept and bleak.

"Okay, Jason," said Omar. "It is time to see the African Grand Canyon."

5

It was nothing like the Grand Canyon.

We stopped in a little car park near a bend in the mountain road. A few enterprising people had set up trinket stalls, selling polished pieces of rock and small camels made from clay. Thankfully, there was already another car in place, disgorging a family of French tourists. The peddlers made a beeline for them, realising I would offer meagre pickings. Beyond the stalls was an overgrown patch of scrub that looked down into the valley below. As far as views went, it was okay, but hardly evocative of Arizona's main attraction. It looked more like a brown quarry.

What was more interesting was a forgotten memorial hidden in the scrub. Nobody else had noticed it. I looked at the faded copper plate nailed to the lump of white rock. It read: *Bernard Borrel, Magistrat, 27.02.1955 – 18.10.1995.* Borrel's story is an odd one.

Bernard Borrel was a Frenchman working in Djibouti City as a judge. He was married with two young children and, in the mid-90s, his job entailed him working with high-ranking Djiboutian minsters in an attempt to overhaul their antiquated justice system. Borrel's main obstacles were government officers who thought that any changes to the system might curtail their underhand methods. Put simply, they believed their cushy way of life would cease. These stumbling blocks became such a drain on Mr Borrel's working life that he requested a transfer out of Djibouti to a different country. And this is where things become a little confused.

While waiting for his transfer, Borrel allegedly withdrew $8000 from his bank account. He hid the cash in an envelope that also contained a letter to his wife. His wife denies this, claiming she never received a letter or the money. Anyway, after hiding the envelope (or not, as the case may be), he drove to a petrol station and purchased a few litres of fuel, collecting it in a jerry can. Then he set off on a long journey that ended at Africa's Grand Canyon, the place where I now stood. After parking his car, Mr Borrel climbed out, calmly removed his shoes and stripped to his underwear and T-shirt. Then he retrieved the jerry can and poured petrol over himself. With one last look into the canyon, he flicked the lighter and threw himself over.

Or did he?

There are massive holes in this apparent suicide, not least of which was why he even wanted to kill himself. After all, he had a wife and two small children, and was probably going to be transferred out of Djibouti soon. Another unusual detail was his method of suicide. Why not simply jump and be done with it? Why go through the rigmarole of buying fuel, stripping off and then setting himself on fire? And why drive all the way to the Djiboutian desert to do it? Surely there were easier ways to take one's life. It was all very strange, especially when a witness claimed he had overheard a presidential advisor talking about the 'elimination of the prying judge' and that 'no traces remained'. The plot thickened when this alleged advisor turned out to be the President of Djibouti (he has since been cleared of any charges). Furthermore, a documentary aired in 2002 claims that Borrel could not have committed suicide in the way presented by the Djiboutian authorities. Evidence exists, they say, that shows that Borrel's body had blunt weapon trauma on the arm and skull. Did he whack himself with a hammer before pouring the petrol? No, they say, a third party was involved, and his wife agrees. She is still trying to get to the bottom of what happened.

6

"The earth's crust is very thin here," said Omar. "Maybe only two or three miles thick." We had driven for a few more miles and pulled into the side of the road. To our left the land was arid and rocky, bounded by a few hills; to our right were the beginnings of the salt lake: small beige outcrops and large boulders jutting above shallow water. White glistened at their edges: salt.

I followed Omar towards the higher ground on my left, skirting the side of a hill. After fifty metres or so, we stopped by a small, shallow pool of clear water that lapped against a rocky cliff.

"Seventy degrees Celsius," said Omar, crouching down next to it. "The earth heats it up." He dipped his finger in and out. He gestured that I should do the same, which I did. It was like sticking my finger into a cup of hot coffee.

"Just below us is hot magma. This is where it gets close to the surface. Later I will show you a fumarole, an opening to the magma, and then a lava tunnel. We can walk through it. But first, we will see the lake."

The road took us further downwards and, in the distance, I caught my first glimpse of the great body of water. It shimmered in the heat haze of a burgeoning African afternoon, a kaleidoscope of gorgeous aquamarines and turquoises, edged with a rim of pure white: the salt deposits for which the lake was famous. Waves rippled across its edge.

We passed a large orange JCB, and then a digger: both Chinese models, I noted. Gangs of local men were huddled at the edge of the road clearing sand and digging holes under the supervision of a Chinese man.

"The Chinese are interested in the salt," explained Omar. "Eventually, they will have factories that will take the salt from the lake so they can sell it. They paid for the road we are travelling on so they can move it by truck. Not far from here, they are building their own port."

I wasn't really listening to him; instead, I was gazing at the sheer majesty of Lake Assal. No photo could ever do it justice. It stretched to the horizon and, as far as I could tell, contained not a single vessel or creature. As beautiful as it was, it was easy to see why the lake had earned the nickname *Hell.* Surrounded by volcanic peaks and scarred with ridges of darkened basalt, it looked like a place where monsters came to die, which was how French geographer Edgar Aubert de la Rü described it when he clapped eyes on the lake in

1937. Another explorer claimed that demons had sculpted the gorges and canyons that surrounded the lake. And yet, despite all this, it was still beautiful.

Omar and I were walking along a salt-caked path that ended at the water's edge. I stopped to scoop up a handful of shiny white orbs. The salt crystals looked like small pearls, rounded and smoothed by the lake. Closer in, a series of rickety tables offered trinkets for visitors. Large salt pebbles, bags of salt and strange-shaped crystalline forms were all for sale. I was their only customer and walked by them all without lingering. Beyond the stalls was an expanse of cracked white, ending at the water. We crunched across it, with wind whipping around my head, as if a demonic force had unleashed itself across Lake Assal.

"Why is it so windy?" I asked.

Omar gestured all around. "Because there is nothing to stop it. We are sitting in the centre of a volcanic bowl, a caldera."

That made sense. A few steps later, Omar stopped. "Did you know that normal sea water contains about 35 grams of salt per litre? Well, Lake Assal contains ten times that amount. It is very easy to float without effort. Are you going in?"

I shook my head. As tempting as it was on such a hot day, I hadn't brought my swimming things. Besides, I'd already wallowed in the Dead Sea and a man-made saline pond in the United Arab Emirates. Floating about in Djibouti just didn't really float my boat. But the view was spectacular, a panorama of salt crystals and picture-perfect blue water. I decided to wade into the lake. Omar joined me in the warm soupy froth and dipped his finger into the water, tasting it. I did too and found it hellishly salty, as if I'd shaken a salt dispenser onto my tongue. Omar went one further and picked up a lump of salt. After licking it, he threw it back in.

"This lake was part of the salt caravan," he told me. "The Afar people came here with their camels to collect salt bricks. Then, when they were fully loaded, they would set off across the desert towards Ethiopia. They still do this, but on a much smaller scale."

I waded back to the white shore and turned to look at the water once more. Instead of hell, it looked like heaven, albeit a horrendously hot version of it. Omar and I crunched our way back to Abdur and the waiting Toyota.

7

We drove to a volcanic beach for lunch. A threadbare cafe was at one end, overlooking a beautiful inlet of the Gulf of Aden. Instead of the yellow of sand, it was a dirty grey colour: residue from the volcanoes. I was the only patron of the cafe and, while Omar and Abdur went inside the concrete building to chat with the owner, I sat outside facing the sea. I could feel my head cold getting worse, causing sneezes and the beginnings of a sore throat, but the view cheered me: a gorgeous line of blue that ended on the horizon at some ominous black peaks.

On my left were a few palm-covered huts, and, while I waited for lunch to arrive, I wandered over to inspect them. Each was about the size of a large tent, bare inside except for fabric bed mattresses. If I'd been inclined, I could have slept in one of them for the night, as tourists sometimes did.

My lunch came, a foil-wrapped fish sandwich. While I ate it, a 4x4 arrived and parked on the beach further down. A western man got out and dragged a surfboard parasail into the water. Soon after, he was deftly catching the currents to twist and glide over the surface of the water. Just then, Omar arrived and sat opposite me, blocking my view slightly. "How is the food?"

I nodded and murmured enjoyment.

"And how about the trip so far?"

I told him the truth: that I was enjoying myself, far more than I'd expected too, as it happened. "This," I said, sweeping my arm around the whole area, "is why tourists should come to Djibouti. Forget the city and come to the desert."

"Maybe you should be a nomad."

I pointed at the parasailer. "He looks like he's having fun."

Abdur watched him for a while. "He will be a solider based in Djibouti City. This will be his day off."

Half an hour later, we were back on the road, Abdur was munching on a fresh batch of khat as we headed towards the lava fields. As we passed through a small canyon, Abdur slowed the car down. We stopped near a gap in the cliffs. Jagged black rock towered over us, but, through the opening in the escarpment, we could see a carpet of black and brown serrated volcanic rock stretching all the way to a distant mountain. We climbed out to look closer.

"That mountain is the volcano that erupted in 1978. Its name is Ardoukoba," Omar told me. I squinted my eyes to see it. Instead of being a classic cone shape, it was long and flat-topped. It looked more like a compressed hill than a volcano. It was hard to imagine that it was responsible for all the field of lava in front of me. It must have literally blown its top off. I questioned Omar about this.

"The lava is not just from that eruption. There have been many more before it." He turned around and pointed out something in the road: a crack. It wasn't enough to stop a car, or even a bicycle, but it was still noticeable. We walked over to it. "It is growing every year," Omar told me, "And this side is *Asian* Africa." He stepped to the other side, uphill from the gap. "And this side is *Black* Africa. In a few million years, there will be an ocean separating where we now stand."

And with that thought rumbling around my head, we headed back to the car.

8

Abdur was grappling with the steering wheel, negotiating us along a rough track that meandered between gigantic volcanic boulders and baked black basalt. With a surge of power, we cleared a peak of rough terrain, my teeth shaking in their sockets as the seat pummelled my backside. Outside, there was nothing except lava and dust. Even the main road was a long way behind us, unseen behind a high plateau. Eventually we came to a standstill. The landscape looked blackened and desolate. Ruptured slabs of dark rock lay scattered around a land of fire and brimstone. I could imagine a pterodactyl rising from within. Or maybe a dragon. Those early explorers were right about this part of Djibouti, I realised; it was hotter than hell, and as parched as the Devil's bedroom, the swirling wind baking everything dry.

Omar said, "Now it is time for the fumaroles. Come, follow me."

I tailed him up a rocky lava outcrop, scrambling over black rocks like a mountain goat. Almost at the top, Omar stopped and pointed to a large rock. It looked like all the others, except that a smaller rock, about the size of a shoe, lay snug on top. Omar lifted the smaller rock and gestured that I should feel the air coming out. I did. It was hot on my hand, like air escaping from an oven. "This is the fumaroles. Down there is the magma," Omar intoned.

I moved to peer into the chasm, but there was nothing to see except blackness; besides, the heat was stinging my eyes. "Maybe today, it will erupt again," I said, half-jokingly.

"I do not think so. The volcanoes are sleeping now. Anyway, we would know if one was about to erupt because the earth would be shaking."

Omar replaced the slab and we climbed back down. He led me to another patch of lava that appeared to be a small crater. When Omar climbed over the rim and disappeared, I looked over. He was gone, clambering into a small cave. I climbed down after him, glad of my long trousers and thick shoes against the sharp edges and textured ground. Then I realised it wasn't a cave; it was far too symmetrical. It was a lava tunnel.

Omar was waiting for me, some distance in. I caught up in an area of the tunnel large enough for us both to stand up in. Sunlight entered via cracks and holes in the roof. "Lava flowed through here," said Omar. "It flowed from the magma chamber and, if we were inside when it happened, we would see an orange river. Then we would be dead."

I took it all in. I had never been inside a lava tunnel before, and hadn't realised that visiting one was part of my Lake Assal tour. I asked Omar how far it went.

"Long way," he answered. "Eventually it goes down into the earth to the magma chamber."

"How deep?"

"Maybe ten kilometres." Suddenly, he raised his hand and gestured that I should be quiet. He tilted his head and then touched the side of the tunnel. "Did you feel that?"

"Feel what?"

"The tremble. And the heat." Omar looked worried. "Not good. Hot gases might be coming …"

Before my own hot gases could escape, Omar erupted into laughter. He guffawed like a hyena and I did too. "I joke with you," he said. "I am very sorry."

We made our way out of the tunnel into the bleak landscape beyond. Abdur was smoking another cigarette. All was well in Djibouti. And now it was time to leave the land of volcanoes and drive back to the city.

Clockwise from top left: The beauty of Lake Assal; Nomads in the Djiboutian hinterland; Omar holding a bunch of khat; Me posing on a beach of salt; A gazelle standing upon Djibouti's bleak volcanic landscape

Chapter 3: Port Louis, Mauritius

Leaving Djibouti was easier than arriving. Just a stamp and that was it. The Ethiopian Airlines turboprop lifted me from the runway into another balmy African morning. Ten minutes later, a bag of peanuts came my way, but I ignored it in favour of the view outside. The dust that coated Djibouti city was borne below me, transported across the Horn of Africa on a harsh wind.

Half an hour later, we were on the ground in a place called Dire Dawa. It was a brief stop to allow a few passengers off before we took off for Addis Ababa. Once there, I climbed out of my seat and grabbed my luggage.

A few days previously, the international departure terminal of Addis Ababa Bole Airport hadn't impressed me, and it did not impress me now. I wandered by the same sorry-looking cafes as I'd done then, passing the same shops selling the same gaudy pieces of fabric and wooden carvings. I made one complete circuit; I made another. With my flight to Nairobi not leaving for another few hours, I was already bored out of my mind.

I hated airports, especially tiny ones such as this. Foreign travel sounded exciting, glamorous even, but not stuck in an airport. And after this airport, I had to contend with one in Nairobi, a place I was spending the night before catching a flight to Mauritius the next day. And so, with nothing better to do, I found a table in one of the cafes and ordered a sandwich.

My food came, and I looked at my watch. Only thirty minutes had elapsed since I'd entered the terminal. I still had one hour and forty minutes to go. Except I didn't. When I chanced a look at an electronic monitor, I saw a delay was marked on the Nairobi flight. I sighed, ate my sandwich and went on another tour of the shops and duty free outlets.

Two hours passed with no update on my flight and so I retired to a reclining chair. With my feet jutting into the walkway, I tried to sleep. Then I felt a whack on my shoe, which startled me awake. It was a cleaner armed with a mop. I moved my feet back to allow her passage. She did so without a word of thanks, and then returned in the opposite direction five minutes later, pulling a face when she had to stop. Once again, I retracted my limbs to allow her past, thinking of the bother of it all. When she started a third sweep of my row, even though it was squeakily clean already, I gave up and retired back to the café – where I remained for the next FOUR HOURS.

Finally, after almost six hours, I boarded my flight to Nairobi.

2

By the time we landed at Nairobi's Jomo Kenyatta International Airport, it was dark, never the best time to arrive in a new country. My cold had given me a bad headache and all I wanted to do was rest

Bearing the scars of my last visit to a Kenyan airport, where a two-hour visa queue had sent me into a rage of despair, I had come prepared with an electronic visa. As I rushed past people dithering with their luggage, I arrived at the back of a single, unruly queue. There were hundreds of people in it. It was already past midnight, I was dog tired, and now this. I coughed in consternation, my chest tightening with the effort.

For ten miserable minutes, I shuffled forward until I managed to read a distant sign. It said: *Anyone who has visited the Middle East, South America or West Africa in the last 14 days: present themselves to the authorities.* I had departed Qatar only four days previously but bugger presenting myself to the mercy of the authorities. I stayed put, idly watching the TV monitors in front of me. Instead of showing movies, they showed infrared images of people in green, yellow and orange. A couple of tripod-mounted cameras were at the head of the line. They were filming our body temperatures for Ebola.

Green seemed okay, but orange or red was bad. The camera lingered on a man ahead of me and paused. He was red and the monitor flashed up his temperature: 37.4 degrees Celsius. This was not high enough for him to be pulled out and imprisoned, and so the camera moved on, searching out any unfortunate who might be trying to bring disease and pestilence onto Kenyan soil.

I felt a cough rising in my chest, but stifled it, aware that if anyone saw me, the cameras would zoom straight in. When they found out I lived in the Middle East, I would be taken outside and shot, I was sure of it. I felt stirrings of alarm and tried to think of a way out. With about a hundred people still in front of me, I had some time to ponder things.

I strained my neck to see the front of the line. Standing underneath the monitors was a stout uniformed woman checking yellow fever certificates. She was busy and overworked. The yellow fever certificate was not an issue, as I had mine in my pocket. The all-seeing electronic eyes were the problem. The line moved forward but then I noticed a few people had bypassed it. They looked like dignitaries or maybe diplomats. An airline crew passed next, and so did a woman who looked Indian. All of them were on the other side of the rope barriers. With wanton abandon, I lifted the rope and joined them. The yellow fever checking woman didn't even notice me. Half an hour later, I was through immigration and sitting in a taxi.

The only thing I can recall about the hotel was the huge fat American man checking in next to me. He was about fifty and sweating profusely. I watched a droplet run down his jowls before it turned towards the fold of his expansive neck. But that wasn't why I remembered him. I remembered him for the question he asked the young check-in girl.

"Hey, miss," he drawled. "Do you know any place where I can get a ... you know ... a massage? A real one ... if you catch my meaning."

I wondered if the young woman was as disgusted as I was. If she was, then she didn't show it. She simply said she didn't know. As for me, I walked to the lift, weary and fed up. Travel was supposed to be fun, and full of exciting things happening. I retired into my room and fell asleep.

3

The large Air Mauritius Airbus took us over the eastern coast of Africa, then skirted the northern reaches of Comoros and Madagascar before delivering us above the island of Mauritius four hours later. Instead of being the lush tropical paradise I'd expected, it looked like the west coast of Ireland: misty and damp, with sporadic coastal settlements perched on remote cliff tops. If the captain had said, "Good evening from the flight deck. We'll be landing at Cork International Airport in approximately ten minutes," I should not have been surprised.

In the distance was the capital, Port Louis. Due to the approaching sunset, a sprinkling of lights was on show. The city, hugging the coast on the northwest coast, was home to about 150,000 people, making it one of the smallest capitals in the world. My hotel was in the thick of it somewhere but, as we skimmed a final layer of cloud, Port Louis fell behind, leaving a vista of ridges of mountains that marked the centre of the island. Beneath them lay a series of lakes glistening in the fading African sun. Then we were flying over a rolling patchwork of dull green and brown fields that led us to the runway of Sir Seewoosagur Ramgoolam International Airport. When the wheels touched down, it marked the start of phase two of my African adventure.

4

Growing up in 1970s England, my best friend was Kevin Appadoo. Kevin was as English as I was, except that his parents hailed from Mauritius. Aged about eight, Kevin told me he and his family were flying back to the home country to visit his grandparents, people he had never met. A few days after he had gone, I grabbed our family atlas to find out exactly where Mauritius was, surprised to find it off the coast of Africa, near the exotic-sounding Madagascar. For some reason, I'd presumed Mauritius to be in the Caribbean somewhere. I closed the atlas and forgot all about Mauritius.

When the Appadoos returned a few weeks later, Kevin invited me around to his house, saying he had brought something back for me. When I pulled up on my bike five minutes later, Kevin was already sitting on his doorstep with something I didn't even know existed: sugar cane. He passed me a tube of the strange yellow-green vegetation and asked me to taste it. To my eight-year-old taste buds, that piece of sugar cane was the greatest thing I had ever tasted. It was as if a wizard had flicked a wand over a boring stick to create something unbelievable. Over three decades later from that childhood episode, I was finally visiting the country of its origin.

Darkness had descended by the time I cleared the airport. I jumped in a taxi as spots of drizzle started pitter-pattering on the windscreen. "First time in Mauritius?" asked the rotund driver, a bald man in his late fifties.

I told him it was.

"Here on holiday or business?"

"Holiday."

The driver nodded and we set off

The highway was modern and largely free of traffic, probably due to the relatively late hour. Unlike the honking and crumbling roads of Djibouti City, Mauritius was back to the real world of modern cars, efficient roundabouts and speed cameras. My driver had a dashboard device that warned him whenever one was coming up.

The wipers were steadily swishing back and forth, clearing the tropical rain on his windscreen, but the side windows were clear. I looked out at an advertisement for a McDonald's Value Meal, and then a neon sign belonging to a large building called MBC. It stood for the Mauritius Broadcasting Corporation, the country's largest TV company, founded by Sir Seewoosagur Ramgoolam, the same man for whom the airport was named.

Sir Seewoosagur Ramgoolam is a popular man in Mauritius. He was the country's first president, and he cemented his popularity by setting up old age pensions, decreeing that hospitals should offer free healthcare and by making sure children received free education. When he died in 1982, the people of Mauritius went on a naming spree, giving numerous public institutions in the country his name, including the airport, the botanical garden, a college and an old people's home. They didn't stop there. The bespectacled man is on every Mauritian coin in circulation.

Suddenly, without warning, a motorcyclist rocketed out in front of us from a slip road. Either he hadn't seen us or, if he had, he was a daredevil of the highest order. My driver did the only thing possible: he slammed on his brakes.

Instantaneously, we fishtailed, skimming along on a tiny film of water with no control whatsoever. What made it worse was our momentum: we were closing in on the motorcycle's rear wheel. How we missed him, I'll never know, but somehow we did. My laptop was on the floor and so was the driver's phone. The motorcyclist was pulling away, unaware that he had almost been killed.

"Young people," said the driver, visibly shaken by the ordeal. "They do not realise the danger."

I concurred. But I had probably been the same in my teens. The rest of the journey to Port Louis was without mishap or calamity.

5

The next morning, Mauritius looked how it should: green, tropical and sunny. My hotel was at one end of Le Caudan Waterfront, a showy area of upmarket hotels, bars and restaurants. The waterfront also housed the Blue Penny Museum, which contained one of the rarest stamps in the world.

I found the museum easily enough; its home was a nicely restored port office building. Downstairs concerned itself with the history of the island, by way of model ships, old maps and information boards.

Upstairs was the treasure room, housing the fabled Penny Blue, a stamp so rare that if I stole it, I would be a millionaire four times over.

Because of its fragility, the stamp is contained within a darkened glass cabinet that only illuminates for ten minutes every hour. I had fifteen minutes to wait, so read about some history. I discovered that as well as the Penny Blue, Mauritius produced another stamp: the Penny Red. Both featured the head of Queen Victoria and were similar to England's more famous Penny Black. Five hundred of each were printed, many ending up on invitations sent out by the Governor of Mauritius for a grand ball. Of the one thousand stamps produced, only 27 remain. Private collectors own most. The Blue Penny Museum was one of the few places on Earth where members of the public could view the stamps.

With five minutes before show time, a few more people arrived and soon there was a crowd. Even though I had arrived first, I had to fight for position at the glass cabinet. And then, at the appointed time, the light came on and, not one, but two illuminated stamps were there for us to coo over: a tiny Penny Blue and an equally tiny Penny Red, both identical apart from the colour. It was all a bit of a letdown, really. Not being a philatelist, I escaped soon after.

Outside, I was walking along a main road full of modern skyscrapers, banks and shopping centres. Downtown Port Louis looked fine, dandy and well run. Behind the skyline, towering above everything, were verdant and tropical hills that eventually formed themselves into highlands seen in the centre of the country. Nowadays, Port Louis is a world away from the mosquito-ridden slave centre from which it started.

The Dutch were the first European settlers to bring slaves to the island, working them on their small-scale plantations. When the French took over, they brought more slaves into Mauritius, mainly from East Africa, to toil in their sugar cane fields. When the British took the island in 1810, they continued with slavery until it was abolished a quarter of a century later. However, with this sudden loss of labour, they devised something called the 'Great Experiment,' whereby Indian paupers, with little prospects at home, were offered the chance of a new life abroad. In return for their passage to the British colonies, they had to work without pay for up to five years. Then they could go back home.

Most of these Indian indentured workers arrived in Port Louis bewildered and fatigued. After disembarking, they were contained within a sprawling centre that became known as Aapravasi Ghat, a Hindu translation of 'Immigration Depot'. Up to one thousand men at time – for it was mostly men whom the English had hoodwinked with the promise of a better life – waited for whatever fate was in store for them. Many were quickly shipped off to Fiji, Malaysia, the West Indies and South Africa: wherever cheap labour was needed. The ones who remained were signed off to work in Mauritian sugar cane plantations.

Aapravasi Ghat is now a World Heritage site by the marina in Port Louis. The complex houses a loose collection of colonial buildings, and I was surprised to find myself the only tourist there. Down by the water's edge, alongside a long jetty, a narrow set of stone steps led up to the main buildings. The steps were the first thing people saw when they arrived by ship. What they must have thought as they climbed them was anyone's guess. I climbed them too, finding myself wandering around some restored buildings: the guardhouse, the infirmary, a kitchen and a depressingly small and dimly-lit shed that had once housed men waiting to be processed. By the time the Great Experiment ended in 1923, hundreds of thousands of Indian workers had passed through Mauritius, with only 25,000 remaining on the island. Today, almost seventy percent of the Mauritian population are descendants of these immigrant workers.

6

Instead of litter and grime, Port Louis had rubbish bins and freshly painted shop fronts (one called the Blue Penny, I noticed). Grass verges were tidy and clipped, and flowers had been planted with thoughtfulness. Men in Port Louis did not lounge about in doorways: they walked with purpose. Shiny cars beeped their way through the bottleneck that formed one of the main streets – a thoroughfare that would have looked ordinary except for the forest of planted palms running through the centre. Port Louis was Africa, but an easy version of it.

Before I left the waterfront, I stopped underneath a large statue of Sir Seewoosagur Ramgoolam. He stood atop a tall stone plinth, holding a book in one hand. He was wearing his trademark thick-rimmed glasses. Ramgoolam eventually died at the ripe old age of 85, right here in Port Louis. His gaze was fixed towards the centre of the city, and I chose to go in the same direction, hoping to locate the capital's most famous area of greenery, Jardin de la Compagnie.

I found it tucked away between a large insurance building and a cash-and-carry. At night, the garden was the haunt of drug dealers, the shade offered by multi-trunked banyan trees perfect for their illicit deals. And with them, plying their ancient trade beneath the dangling branches, were the city's prostitutes. Jardin de la Compagnie was a place to avoid after dark.

At eleven in the morning, it was perfectly safe. People were sitting on benches or passing through on their way to somewhere else. The banyan trees towered over the far reaches of the garden, their spindly branches dangling like jungle snakes. Along the central paved path were a few statues of men I did not recognise. Small benches at the edge offered shade and rest. I sat on one, watching the people passing through: a man wearing a suit, an older man carrying a walking cane, a couple of teenage girls with mobile phones and then a trio of male office workers, presumably taking an early lunch break. I looked in my guidebook for what else there was to see in Port Louis, and discovered the central market, a sprawling district that promised colour and haggling, was only a short walk away.

The start of the market was easy to find due to the number of people heading there, or leaving with bags and boxes of goods. None of the bags was plastic, I noticed. Since the start of the year, Mauritius has banned plastic bags, something more countries should do. I found the main market building along a hectic street of stalls whose produce and goods were spilling into the pavement. But it wasn't all fruit and vegetables: two puppies were sitting patiently inside a small shoebox, peering up at passers-by, hoping someone would stop and pluck them away from the rotten apples and banana skins.

Inside the market hall, I took in the aroma of mangos, apples, oranges, chillies, grapes and bananas. It was a frenzied place of weighing, prodding and sniffing. I walked along the main aisle, watching local men and women haggling over lychees and pineapples or nodding towards ripe papayas. If I had so desired, I could have bought three lemons for 20 rupees (40p) or a single pomelo for 60 rupees.

Opposite was a meat market. I saw I had missed the rush: each of the individual sections was mostly empty. One section was for pork, another specialised in beef. A third was for chicken, but I ignored it in favour of the goat section. Inside, I found men clearing up counters and swishing water across the floor. A few goat carcasses still dangled from hooks with strips of meat laid out underneath. The most gruesome exhibit was a severed goat head lying on a blood-drenched cloth. For some unfathomable reason, someone had peeled its skin off, leaving a red mess of sinew and flesh. Two glassy eyes gazed emptily upwards, and suddenly the smell of blood caused my stomach to lurch. I fled into the sunlight.

7

I spied the dodo through a metal fence. It was yellow with a black head and black rump. There was another one nearby, this one blue. Both sat still and silent in the grounds of a fetching peach coloured colonial. Lettering on the front of the building claimed it was the Mauritius Institute, which also doubled as the Natural History

Museum. I had no time to visit and so gazed back at the dodos. They were about a metre tall (as they were in real life), and *were* distinctly odd-looking. Their elongated beaks and obese bodies made them resemble oversized and especially ugly turkeys.

Long before the first people arrived on Mauritius, these unusual birds had lost their capability for flight. But they didn't need to fly because they had no predators. That all changed when Dutch sailors arrived with their dogs, rats and rifles. After naming them 'dodaars', Dutch for 'fat arse', the sailors sought to capture, cook and eat them in huge quantities. One naval officer wrote that Mauritius was full of 'foules twice as bigge as swans ... being of very good meat.' Others were less complimentary about dodo meat, describing it as unsavoury and tough. Even so, by 1693, less than a century after the first human settlers had arrived in Mauritius, the dodo was no more.

Of all the dodos that have ever lived, only four portions remain. A dried head belongs to the British Museum. They used to have a foot but lost it. Mind you, it is a wonder they still have the head. In 1755, the museum had been the proud owner of an entire bird in stuffed form – the only full Dodo in the world, no less – and yet it was thrown into a fire in the mistaken belief it was a mouldy piece of junk. Only the quick thinking action of a museum employee saved the head and foot. As for the other three pieces, a museum in Denmark has a skull, and a museum in Prague has a piece of Dodo jaw and leg bone. And that is it.

8

I passed through Chinatown. Chophouses, convenience stores, dangling ducks and hardware stores crammed both sides of the busy road. Skilled Chinese workers had starting coming to Mauritius at the end of the eighteenth century, setting up shops that repaired shoes or clothes for the locals. Some of them could tinker with broken machinery and make it work again. Over time, their skill and worth ethic made them wealthy businessmen. Today, they own most of the shops in Port Louis, and make up three percent of the population.

I turned uphill, passing the quite exquisite Jummah Mosque – a nineteenth century building bedecked in white, with arches, fancy wooden doors and small minarets adding decoration. I was on my way to Fort Adelaide, which sat atop of one of Port Louis' many hills. To get there I had to pass a whole line of street hawkers selling sunglasses, ornaments and tourist jumble. Though tempted to buy some sunglasses, I ignored the salesmen, who grew more insistent the steeper the gradient became. Eventually, though, they fell away, leaving me to stumble upon a weed-strewn set of stone steps. By the time I reached the top, I was battling burning lungs and a mutinous heart. When a tour bus pulled up a minute later, filled with day-trippers from the resort hotels, I made my way to the fort entrance, licking my bone-dry lips.

The British built Fort Adelaide in the 1840s to serve as a lookout point across the harbour. It also housed troops and stores, and possessed a secret underground tunnel that led straight to the sea. When vigilant watchmen noticed unknown ships arriving, they would give the signal to send soldiers rushing down to meet them.

Before going inside, I regarded the old fortress. It was large and rectangular with thick tall walls blackened by tropical grime. In its heyday, no one would have called it pretty; in fact, the biggest compliment I could give it was that it looked *functional*. Today, tourists do not visit the fort for the actual bricks and mortar, but rather for the views it offers.

I made my way through an entranceway, finding myself inside a wide courtyard. Instead of barracks and guardrooms, the lower tier contained gift shops, a cafe and a couple of cannons. There was even a young man dressed up in a colonial red uniform and white helmet with a mock rifle strapped to his back. A Japanese woman wearing a floppy straw hat was posing next to him while her boyfriend took a photo.

I climbed the steps to the second level to take in the view. As promised, it was fantastic, covering the whole of the port area, the adjacent skyscraper district and, by looking in the opposite direction, the mountains. Below me, on my right, was the huge oval-shaped track belonging to the Champ de Mars Racecourse. Race days were highly popular in Port Louis, I knew, helped mainly because horseracing is Mauritius' favourite sport. The owners, the Mauritius Turf Club, hold the honour of being the oldest horseracing club south of the Equator. Today, the track looked empty.

I gazed out towards the ocean, taking in Mauritius. I could see why people returned over and over to the island: it really was beautiful, especially away from the noise of the capital. But now it was time to climb down to street level. I had an appointment with a sun lounger. Why travel all the way to a tropical paradise if I couldn't take advantage of it?

9

Because my hotel catered mainly for business people, I had the small beach to myself. I chose a sun lounger close to the bar and ordered a bottle of Phoenix Beer. When it came, I sipped my cold drink, relishing the view. Directly in front of me, almost within touching distance of my toes, was a sliver of water that separated me from the main waterfront complex. A couple of pleasure craft were moored a little further along. But to my left was something more interesting, if not quite so easy on the eye. Sixteen individual, but gigantic, tubes, all connected into one silo-like construction, formed a structure called the Bulk Sugar Terminal.

The memories of my childhood sugar cane tasting roared back to life. Refined sugar from sugar cane, similar to the one I'd savoured, was contained in vast quantities inside the cylinders. When a ship arrived at the terminal, sugar could flow into its hold at a rate of 1450 tonnes per hour, which is a lot of sugar. 1450 tonnes meant twenty-four tonnes per minute, almost half a tonne per second. That is a staggering amount of sugar, which means that Mauritius must be producing insane amounts of sugar. Using the hotel's Wi-Fi, I decided to look into this, staggered to discover that eighty percent of all arable land in Mauritius is set aside for sugar cane production. I decided I wanted to see some of these sugar cane fields myself. I finished my drink and, after half an hour of lazing around, I arranged a tour to the northern part of the island.

Clockwise from top left: Le Caudan Waterfront, one of the nicest parts of Port Louis; A dodo in the centre of the city; Port Louis central market; The hazy skyline of Nairobi from my brief time there; Looking towards the centre of Port Louis

Chapter 4: Sugar Cane, Beaches and Corruption

Francis was in his late fifties, balding badly and in possession of a paunch: a look I would no doubt replicate in fifteen or so years. I shook hands and sat alongside him in his car.

"So you want to see some of the sights of Northern Mauritius? Well, the first place to see is the sugar factory."

"Does it have sugar cane?"

"Plenty. Lots of sugar cane grows in the fields near the factory. I will stop the car so you can see."

As we drove away from the hotel, Francis told me he first became a taxi driver in 1982. "Back then, everything in Mauritius was cheap. Families could live well and raise their children. Not like now. Everything is expensive: food, cars, houses. I am lucky because my wife and I don't have children. I don't know how people survive if they do."

We were passing the old Post Office building, another colonial-era structure. Over on my right I could see Fort Adelaide, jutting out above a line of commercial buildings. On the opposite side of the road was the city's bus station. Unlike most of Port Louis, it was grubby and full of fumes. About ten large buses sat waiting for passengers. Milling around one of them was a collection of old ladies wearing colourful dresses and hats. One guffawed and tapped another playfully on the arm.

"Even fish is expensive in this country," said Francis, shaking his head at this seemingly absurd fact. "And we are an island surrounded by ocean! It is not right." He explained that the hotels bought most of the island's daily stock, driving up prices for the locals. "That is why I went to work in France for ten years. I got a construction job in Paris. I saved lots of money. I enjoyed France, but living there made me realise how badly the government runs Mauritius. You can probably guess why."

"Corruption?" I hazarded.

Francis nodded solemnly.

I was soon to discover that corruption was Francis's favourite subject, but for now, with the outskirts of Port Louis firmly behind us, we turned towards the sugar factory. Fields of sugar cane, far taller than the car, flanked both sides of the road. I mentioned to Francis about my old friend from Mauritius, and how his parents had moved to England in the late sixties.

"They did the right thing. They would be sad to see what has happened to our country."

We pulled over and I climbed into the forest of sugar cane. They dwarfed me, perhaps nine feet tall. These specimens were thicker than the one I'd sampled all those years ago, and each cane had extensive and luxuriant leaves sprouting from the top. But I still recognised it, and found a section of broken tube on the ground. I rubbed it free of dry soil and snapped it in half. It was so strong I had to use all my might. Then I stuck the end in my mouth and chewed on the pulpy mess. Immediately my taste buds were rewarded with a mad sugar rush, as if I'd licked a spoonful of sugar. To my adult senses, this was not nice, and I grimaced. How different from when I'd been a child.

2

We pulled into a spare bay in the car park. An empty tour bus was parked nearby, plus a few cars, hinting that the L'Adventure du Sucre was not going to be the working sugar factory I'd hoped for. Francis told me he would wait in the car for me. "Take your time," he said, picking up a newspaper. "There is no rush." I nodded and walked towards the main building.

After paying the entrance fee, I headed inside the self-declared adventure, finding it to be exactly what I feared: a museum full of old photographs and paintings, dangling bags of sugar, restored machinery and information boards explaining it all. I gave most of it only a cursory glance, but I did learn that sugar cane is actually a type of grass, and that it is the world's most harvested crop, if measured by quantity.

I caught up with a tour group, presumably from the coach. They were huddled around an exhibit displaying a large sugar cone. I listened as their guide explained that the bullet-shaped lump of white was a handy way of transporting the stuff on ships. I walked off, finding another large group loitering near a mock-up of a sugar transportation ship. One man, clearly bored out of his skull, watched me with envy as I skipped past the wooden vessel to enter the final section of the museum – the obligatory gift shop.

Fridge magnets, key rings, cuddly dodo toys and bottles of New Grove Rum were waiting for me. I wasn't interested in any of it and walked straight up to the tiny bar tucked in the corner. My entry ticket included a free sample of New Grove, made by the factory. If I liked it, I could then buy a bottle. I handed over my ticket and the woman behind the counter offered me three choices: dark, white or spiced. I opted for spiced. She nodded and poured the most meagre of measures into a thimble-sized glass. A gnat would have difficulty getting drunk on it. Anyway, I necked off the brown liquid in a split second, grimaced and then went to find Francis.

He seemed surprised to see me. He closed his newspaper. "Have you been inside the museum?"

I nodded. "I've been around the whole thing."

Francis looked at his watch. "But you have only been in for fifteen minutes. I've only read four pages of my newspaper. That must be a world record."

I didn't know whether to be proud or embarrassed: probably the latter. I climbed into the passenger seat for the next part of the tour.

3

As we drove back through the sugar cane fields, Francis started talking about corruption again, and gave me some prime examples. "If you want your car fixed, you take it to a repair shop and wait a long time, unless ..." Francis looked at me and nodded knowingly, "... unless you pay a little bit under the table. Then they will fix your car quickly. It's the same with a house. You find a plot of land in a nice area, then you wait for a long time – maybe years – until the government gives you permission to build on it. But if you pay the backhander, then it might only take a few weeks. What if your passport needs renewing? It will take a long time, unless you are prepared to pay the bit on the side. Money is king in Mauritius. It turns all the cogs and greases every wheel."

I murmured consolation, which gave Francis an excuse to carry on. "You need a new permit to drive a bus ... pay a little bribe and the permit is yours. It doesn't even matter if you cannot drive, as long as you have money, they do not care. Corruption is rife. And do you know who is to blame? Yes, the politicians. They take their cut while the poor man gets poorer. That is why crime is rising in Mauritius: the underclass has had enough."

I nodded in sympathy, but couldn't really add anything to what he was saying; I simply didn't know enough about Mauritius. All I knew was that it had a decent airline, an efficient transport system and, as far as I could tell, a working infrastructure.

"Tell me, have you heard of Seewoosagur Ramgoolam?"

I told Francis I had.

"Well his son is called Navin Ramboolam. He has been the Prime Minister of Mauritius three times and, last year, he was arrested for money laundering. It is not the first time he has been arrested! His father would turn in his grave if he knew."

"Well, if he was arrested, it means they are doing something about it."

Francis shook his head. "You do not understand. The only reason he was arrested was that he was caught with his fingers in the pie. Everyone is at it. As much as I hate saying this about the country of my birth, I do not see how things can get any better. Corruption is a way of life here. And it always will be."

We turned off a roundabout and arrived at the Seewoosagur Ramgoolam Botanical Garden, the oldest botanical garden in the southern hemisphere, according to Francis. A series of stalls was just outside the fence: one stall was selling fruit, another drinks. I went to buy some water while Francis parked the car. "Have fun, Jason. And this time, let me read my newspaper. There is an article about insurance scams in Mauritius."

4

The botanical garden turned out to be great. It was a massive area of plants, ponds and creatures. The creatures were small deer and giant tortoises (housed in pens) and stunning red finches that whipped around the treetops with noisy chirps. I found a lily pond and stared at the huge green circles in the water. Only a frog leaping between them would have made the scene better. And though the garden (which was nothing like a garden in the traditional sense – for a start, it was more like a jungle forest in places) was full of tourists, it was still possible to find quiet, secluded parts to get in touch with some tropical nature.

At one point in my wanderings, a secondary school geography lesson came into mind. In it, the teacher, a wizened ex-army sergeant, was teaching us how temperate and tropical climates differed. The only thing I could recall about the lesson was that some trees in the tropics had buttress roots. Well, he was right, because I was staring right at some: extra surface roots that, as well as searching out nutrients, offered support to the tree to which they belonged.

One section of the garden was full of trees planted by visiting dignitaries. The King of Swaziland had planted an African Black Ebony tree in May 2000. It looked healthy and well cared for. The president of Zambia had planted a bushy specimen called Cordia sebestena; it was double my height. Both were better than the effort planted by Alberto Chissano, president of Mozambique. The sapling he had planted in 1993 was no longer there; only a bare patch of grass remained in its place. I carried on walking, finding Robert Mugabe's tree, a Gastonia Mauritania, massive and thriving, and far healthier than one planted by the president of the Maldives. Even though it was over five years old, the thing was only a few inches high: a tiny sapling with only a scant offering of needle-like branches. What made it worse was the mighty piece of wood from China opposite. It was the tallest tree along the avenue.

I heard a waterfall. I peered around bushes and through trees but couldn't see any sign of it. Then the waterfall found me. The heavens unleashed a tropical torrent, soaking the path I was walking upon, drenching me in a breath. I ran in search of shelter, finding refuge under a large palm. In the distance, caught out in the open, a phalanx of tourists ran in all directions, screaming all the way. While I waited, a frog hopped by, eyed me suspiciously and bounded off into the undergrowth. I smiled to myself: the botanical garden had turned out to be an unexpected delight.

Finally, the rain eased, and I left my hiding place, finding that the temperature had cooled. With a newfound spring in my step, I located the exit and walked towards the waiting car.

5

As Francis and I drove further north, we passed a policeman armed with a speed camera. Francis grumbled something and shook his head. "Another prime example of corruption."

He went on to explain.

"Imagine I'm driving along, minding my own business, and that policeman stops me. First, he writes me a speeding ticket, or maybe a ticket for not indicating properly. To pay this ticket means taking a lot of time out from my day. I need to go to this office, that office, see this official, and get a stamp from the captain: all hassle I do not need. But the policeman has another way – and this has happened to me many times. He gives me the ticket and I fold a two-hundred rupee note inside. Then I pass it back to him. The policeman will look, nod his head and wave me away, the ticket forgotten."

Two hundred rupee was about six dollars. Francis second guessed what I was thinking.

"Two hundred is not much, I know, but that policeman – and many more just like him – will stop maybe twenty drivers a day. That means ... four thousand rupees, maybe more, straight into their pockets."

Four thousand rupees was over a hundred dollars a day. I asked how much a policeman earned in Mauritius.

"I'm not sure Maybe about $1200 dollars per month. But with their backhanders, they can earn four or five times that. But it's not just police: court officials, hospital admission officers and even customs officers are in on it, too. I know this because my brother is a customs official. He is so rich that he is building a second house for tourists to rent."

Despite the alleged corruption, the people we were passing looked happy enough. A group of grey-uniformed schoolchildren were hanging around at a bus stop, waiting for one of the large red and white Ashok Leyland buses to pull up. All of them were smiling and joking around. And a group of older women seemed jolly too, wandering along the street with bags of flowers balanced on their heads.

As our conversation quietened, the traffic thickened, as did the number of tourists. Flip-flops, sunglasses and sunburned skin walked along a busy street of cafes, bars and souvenir shops. It looked like Spain, Greece or Turkey. We had arrived in Grand Bay, home to some of the best resorts on the island – the type of place where a couple might spend their honeymoon. Francis told me he would find somewhere to park so I could see the public beach.

He managed to find a tight spot, deftly reversing past a row of motorbikes, a small van and a line of taxis. I got out, taking in the view. It was not quite paradise, but as close to it as a public beach would allow. The beach was clean and golden with small boats sloshing about in the aquamarine water. Underneath the palm trees, a few stray (and harmless) dogs lounged in the shade. At the far end was a fish market. I walked over to it while Francis lit a cigarette. Though there were only about five or six tables, each one was full to bursting with colourful marine creatures. One table had bright orange fish; another had squid. A third was crammed with huge chunks of tuna, each piece larger than my luggage. A man walked up and pointed to a long silver fish, about a metre in length, saying something to the stallholder. The proprietor nodded, grabbed a knife and sliced open the fish's belly. After he removed the innards, he placed the fish back on the table and bagged up the guts. Transaction complete, the man walked away with his bag of fish offal.

I found Francis talking to another man further along the beach. He introduced his pal as his cousin. He looked about forty, with a wiry body and equally wiry black hair. I shook hands and gestured towards the ocean. "You see this every day. You are a lucky man."

He looked at the boats bobbing up and down. "I guess I am."

I asked whether sharks lurked out in the water.

"Of course. But the sharks here are laid back. They see people relaxing and they relax, too. Plus, there's plenty of fish out there for them. Eating a tourist is hard work for these Mauritian sharks. They prefer to swim around, open their mouths a little and then dance with the squid. They are Rasta sharks."

Francis looked at the ocean but seemed less enamoured. Seeing it every day obviously dulled its lustre, I supposed. We headed back to the car for the final stop of my short tour

6

Cap Malherureux is a tiny coastal village located on the northern tip of Mauritius. Its name comes from the French for 'Cape of Bad Luck,' named so because of the British navy attacking them there, plus the fact that the sea around the cape was decidedly rocky, capable of destroying the flimsy hulls of early nineteenth century ships.

The journey there from Grand Bay took about fifteen minutes and, along the way, Francis gave his final talk about corruption. I think he could tell I was tiring of it.

"Mauritius is home to Muslims, Hindus and Christians. Most people are Hindu – about half the population. Christians are next, leaving about twenty percent of the population Muslim. Here's the thing, though – the prime minister of Mauritius is always a Hindu. Always was and always will be. It's just the way it is."

I shook my head in what I hoped was sufficient annoyance at this, even though I had no idea what he was getting at.

"There is a tax rule here in Mauritius that favours Hindus. Not many tourists know this." Francis then actually looked around, as if searching out anyone who might be eavesdropping, even though we were inside a car. He lowered his voice. "If you live in the city or any of the towns, you have to pay tax to the government. This is a lot of money. But – and this is a big but – if you like in a village, you do not pay this tax. Can you guess which group of people mainly live in the villages?"

"Hindus?"

"Exactly. The Prime Minister looks after his own."

"So why don't Catholics and Muslims move to the villages?"

"Because they are not welcome. And besides, they would need special permission from the government. If you are a Christian, or even worse, a Muslim, you stand no chance. Unless, of course, you have money. Cash trumps everything in Mauritius. Anyway, enough of this talk on how my country is falling apart, you don't want to hear me moaning all day."

Cap Malheureux turned out to be another beach village, though a much less touristy one. Out in the Indian Ocean was a series of black outcrops and boulders, rocks that could catch out unobservant mariners, I thought. But the beach wasn't the main sight: a small and daintily painted red-roofed church was. It looked like it belonged on the front of a biscuit tin or, at the very least, a postcard.

7

It was called the Notre Dame Aurilliatrice Chapel. I asked Francis who had built it and how old it was. He looked blankly. "I do not know how old it is. Maybe the French built it. The name sounds French."

Like many places of worship, the outside was better than the interior, but what annoyed me were some Western kids ringing the bells and darting around the pews. The parents seemed unconcerned that their offspring were running rampage around a working church, more interested in the altar. To escape the din, I returned to the beach.

The spot I chose was quiet and free of tourists. While I dithered on the beach, Francis returned to the car, worried about the prospect of rain. On the horizon, beyond the bobbing pleasure craft and fishing boats, lay Coin de Mire Island, a dramatic slab of rock that rose up sharply at one end before tapering almost to sea level at the other. Brooding clouds hovered ominously over it. If time had been on my side, I could have caught a catamaran to the island to wander the remains of an old Dutch sugar plantation or to observe the lizards and birds that lived there. But for now, I was content to stare out at the gentle rolling waves. There was something peaceful about staring at a large body of water, I'd found, and this was no different. It was only when concentric circles started forming in the water, followed by greasy drops on my head, that I made a move for it. I found Francis, who seemed jollier now that corruption was off his chest. On the way back to Port Louis, his mood had increased sufficiently for him to take me on a detour to view his brother's – under construction – house. Because of the rain, we looked at it from inside the car.

"So this was paid for by bribes," I said, wondering whether it would set Francis off again.

"Not all of it. My brother put a lot of his own money into it. Plus, he's paying me to paint it."

I nodded in appreciation at the work that had gone into the house. It had a double parking space, a wide upstairs balcony and plenty of wall-to-wall glass windows. When it was finished, it would also have a swimming pool. It was going to make a fine house.

Twenty minutes later, we pulled up outside the hotel. Just before I climbed out, Francis passed me a business card with his name on the top plus a telephone number. "If you come back with your wife, let me know. I will get you a special deal in a hotel. I'll organise things for you to see. I'll make sure your wife loves Mauritius. And I promise not to talk about corruption."

I took the card, shook his hand and I thanked him for showing me a little bit of his island. I watched as he drove away, thinking of my next destination: Madagascar, only a two-hour flight way from Mauritius.

Clockwise from top left: The quite stunning Grand Bay public beach; The chapel at Cap Malheureux; Lily pads in the botanical garden; A palm overlooks the Indian Ocean; Red Ashok Leyland buses are everywhere in Mauritius; Fish for sale

Chapter 5: Antananarivo: Capital of Madagascar

"You have no visa," the immigration officer at Antananarivo Ivato International Airport stated, already calling the next person to his booth. I'd been waiting in his infernal queue for thirty minutes for him to tell me this.

I stood my ground. "I didn't think I needed one. Can't you just stamp me in?" I hoped the man with the ink would offer a smidgeon of clemency.

"All tourist need visa. Please leave." He was bored out of his mind.

"Can't I get the visa from you?"

"Visa from over there." He pointed back from where I came.

I huffed, and I puffed, and I threw myself down. Except I didn't. I meekly left the man's little booth and walked back into the fray known as Immigration No Man's Land. Here, people wandered lost or confused, and I had already been there. But then I spied the visa counter, a small poky Perspex-fronted stall, which I had previously thought a money exchange. At that particular moment, there was no one waiting and so I rushed forward to claim my place.

"How long you stay?" asked the young woman behind the screen. She was already looking at her phone, flicking through some photos, as bored as the immigration officer.

"Four days," I said.

"Four days? 90,000 ariary please."

I had no idea how much 90,000 ariary was worth and so flashed an American hundred-dollar bill her way. She nodded and took it. After some rummaging, she produced a slip of paper, stamped something in my passport and handed me a wad of Malagasy ariary as change. I found out later that the highest denomination banknote, the 10,000 ariary, was only worth three dollars. And yet among the pile of cash were 100 ariary notes, worth a whopping six cents. So the visa had cost me $27. I stuffed the whole lot into my luggage and then rejoined the immigration queue. After thirty minutes of hateful shuffling, along the same route I'd already taken, I arrived back at the man with the stamp. He checked the visa and then shook his head. "No police stamp."

"What?" I was ready to stamp my feet on a policeman.

"Over there." He pointed at a little booth next to the visa office.

"Really? I've got to go back again? This is insane!"

"Without police stamp over the visa, you cannot enter Madagascar."

Resigned to my fate in this most Godforsaken of tropical airports, I left the line again and headed towards the police counter. On the evidence presented to me thus far, I hated Madagascar like no other country I'd visited.

2

Two hours earlier, I had been gazing down at the landscape of Madagascar, the fourth largest island in the world. Lush-forested highlands, quilted collages of green and brown, it had looked beautiful as it skimmed underneath the wing. Out of all the places on my trip around Africa, Madagascar was the one I was looking forward to most. For a start, it was the promised land of lemurs and chameleons, two of my favourite creatures in the animal kingdom. Then there was the capital, Antananarivo (or Tana, as the locals called it), which was not short of a few sights itself. I was quietly, but supremely, excited.

As we descended further, terraced hills and low-lying paddy fields came into view. Then swathes of tropical palms began a fight for supremacy over eucalyptus trees, the latter introduced in the 1920s and now threatening to take over all the island's indigenous forests. I spied a thick brown river meandering around large patches of brown highland, its floodwater glistening in the afternoon sun. Adjacent fields were waterlogged, for I was arriving into Madagascar at the end of the rainy season, a time of busy rice harvesting. And then the city finally appeared, a sprawling mass of low-level buildings clustered around a series of hills and lakes. From above, Madagascar was exactly what I had hoped for: distinctly African and a thing of beauty. And then I arrived at the airport.

I left the immigration counter for a second time and located the police area. It was a little glass-panelled mini room near the visa counter. I'd noticed it on my way in, but discounted it as unimportant. Well, now I had realised the error of that, and was queuing in yet another line. When I got to the front, a uniformed man took my passport, checked it had a visa inside and then passed it to someone else. The second officer flicked through, checked my visa and passed it to a third man. My passport was on the human conveyor belt of pointlessness, each police officer simply repeating what the one before had done. Eventually, it got to the end of the line where the policeman in charge gave it a stamp. I was free to enter Madagascar.

By the time I was through the other side of the airport, I was strangely serene. There was simply no other way to be in Africa. Even the hustler, a young man who had diligently followed me from the arrivals hall to the taxi stand, all the while pushing an empty luggage cart, failed to arouse my ire. When I climbed into a taxi and refused to pay for a service I did not need (and he did not give), he banged on the window, angry to be losing his windfall. I ignored him and smiled. This made the hustler furious, banging harder until we pulled away.

But I didn't care; I was in Madagascar.

3

Dusty African streets fed away from the airport perimeter. Choking traffic snarled them, including the one upon which we were travelling. I gazed out at a meat stall that specialised in tripe. The one next door had chunks of zebu meat dangling from thin pieces of string. In a darkened alcove, old men toiled over random engine parts. A woman was carrying a massive green melon on her head.

Behind her was an array of fruit and vegetable stalls, then a selection of huts selling handbags. Most of the shacks were made of wood with corrugated metal roofing. When it rained, it must be deafening inside them.

"Is the traffic always this bad?" I asked the driver, a stick-thin young man in a faded red T-shirt. We had been stationary for a few minutes.

The man nodded and then stuck his arm from the window. A boy of perhaps ten ran to him and they exchanged words. The youngster ran off and retuned with a packet of cigarettes. Transaction complete, our car moved on another few metres to where food stalls took over the street.

"Yes. Traffic in Tana always bad," the driver finally said. "More cars every day on the road, but road is not good for this: too thin."

The population of Antananarivo were a mixed bunch. Instead of what I'd expected, many people looked Asian, with a definite hint of Malaysian or perhaps Filipino about them. I thought this was very odd but didn't like to say anything. I noticed a buxom woman in a coloured stripy dress frying food inside a large metal pot of oil. She looked Malay too. I couldn't see what she cooking, but a line of people was waiting for whatever it was. Further on, underneath a pole coiled with wires, sat a group of bored young men with nothing better to do except stare out into the road. Sidestepping them were women carrying bundles on their heads.

The Carlton Hotel was only eighteen kilometres from the airport, yet it took forty-five minutes of gruelling nose-to-nose traffic to pull up outside the self-declared tallest building in Antananarivo (it was actually the third tallest). The exterior looked like a 1970s tower block from a poor estate in urban England (possibly why the Hilton pulled out from running the hotel in 2007), but the interior was plush and expansive. Businessmen sat in the lobby chatting into phones or tapping away on laptops. Well-dressed couples sat in a bar to the side, and rushing hither and thither was an assortment of doormen, bellboys and elevator operators.

My room was almost on the top floor, affording me a grand view of the Malagasy capital. Across from me was Lake Anosy, a large, artificial heart-shaped body of water surrounded by busy roads, jacaranda trees and a steep-sloping hill at its far end. The hill was home to some Hollywood-style white lettering spelling out Antananarivo and, further up, the Rova, the former Malagasy Queen's palace. Although the palace looked statuesque and healthy from my window, I knew this to be untrue, for it was effectively a ruin since a terrible fire had gutted it in 1995. Even so, it was still one of the true worthwhile sights to see in Antananarivo, and one I decided to visit while I had time.

If I thought the traffic was bad from the airport, the narrow lane that led up to the Rova was worse. Built by the French when horses and carts were the main form of transport, it was now a crush of parked cars, which left only a narrow strip for movement. Thank god, the town planners of Tana had made the road one-way only. Without it, there would be gridlock. At the top of the hill, the taxi driver parked near a gate and told me he would wait until I was ready. Through the gate, I could see a portion of the Rova palace.

At the entrance, a few guides and some hawkers trying to sell wooden musical instruments hovered expectantly. As a foreign tourist, I was easy prey for the latter and was under obligation to employ the former. Therefore, my guide around the Rova complex was a wiry man in his early forties called Patrick, who told me he had worked as a palace guide all of his adult life. He could speak four languages. In addition to all the local Malagasy dialects, he was conversant in English, French, Italian and German.

"So this is where the Royal Family lived," said Patrick, gesturing towards the sandstone coloured building in front of us. Even from a short distance away, the fire damage looked minimal; I could not see any blackened brickwork or burn marks. But then Patrick explained that this was because it was under reconstruction and much of the exterior had already been repaired. Before we ventured closer, Patrick told me some more history.

"The first Rova complex was built here in the early 1600s on Antananarivo's highest hill. As well as the palace, the rulers of Madagascar built tombs, chapels and even a place for cock fighting."

"So which king lived here?" I asked.

"Not a king, but a queen. Her name was Queen Ranavalona I. Have you heard of this woman?"

I hadn't, so Patrick told me that she was born in 1778, but she didn't become Queen until fifty years later. During her 33-year reign, she ousted the French from her country, and then set about killing any Christians that came her way. She also worked her subjects so hard that thousands of them died of starvation and disease. And to keep a firm hand over everyone, she used a primitively horrible method of law and order.

Known as a Trial by Tangena, the justice involved the accused party having to prove their innocence by eating a lump of poison extracted from the tangena nut, and three slices of chicken skin. If they died, they were guilty, but if they vomited up all three pieces of skin, they were innocent. It was as simple as that. But the Trial by Tangena wasn't just set aside for serious crimes: petty incidents also went under the poison. For instance, if a householder accused a neighbour of theft, he faced a Trial by Tangena. If someone suspected a woman of being a witch, then she could look forward to a meal of poison and chicken skin. And yet the citizens in Madagascar were happy with this simple form of justice, and indeed often asked for the poison to clear their names. The survival was around fifty percent. Basically, if you scoffed the poison you had a 50-50 chance of being proven innocent.

Even so, during Queen Ranavalona's time at the helm of Malagasy justice, thousands of people died due to tangena poisoning until it was finally outlawed in 1863, consigned to remote rural communities who still swore by it.

5

The Queen's Palace reminded me of a small Tower of London, perhaps due to its square shape and the stout turrets on all four corners. Up close, I could finally see the fire damage; the interior was bare, its windows non-existent and its doors were open to the elements. The Rova palace was a shell. Suddenly, the quiet ambiance was broken by the arrival of a group of blue uniformed schoolchildren. A few looked at me briefly before resuming their rush around the complex, gripping clipboards and trailed by their teacher.

"The fire was bad," Patrick said. "I saw the flames leaping and dancing on the hill and I knew straightaway what was burning. The fire was so bad I could see it from my home in West Tana. When I came to see it a few days later, I almost cried. The damage ..."

"How did it start?" I asked.

"That is a good question. Officially, it was an accident, which I think is odd since the palace didn't have a kitchen, or any place a fire might naturally start. I think the fire was started deliberately." We were walking around the back of the palace, an area favoured by darting skinks. "You see, the Queen's Palace was about to be included in the World Heritage List. If this had happened, important people from other countries would have kept a close eye on it. Maybe some people didn't want them snooping around."

"Why?" We stopped by a wall that offered perhaps the best view of the city: lakes, dwellings and distant hills. Lake Anosy sat in the distance with the Hotel Carlton at its far end.

"You've got to realise that Madagascar is a very corrupt country. People take their cut here and there, fabricate orders, exaggerate prices. The foreigners might notice these things and put a stop to them. Burning the evidence solved that."

I nodded, but still couldn't quite grasp how gutting such a significant historical building could gain anything more than saving the necks of a few incompetents. Surely, a few fiddled accounts or stolen paintings was not as bad as burning everything down. For a start, an intact palace, monitored by the World Heritage, would be a good thing for Madagascar: it would bring in tourists and their hard Western cash.

The guide told me that a few things were saved from the inferno and were now contained in a building a little further along the road that used to be the old Prime Minister's Palace. We walked down a slight hill towards it, passing thin chickens and antique French-built cars parked in dusty driveways. Inside the once grand, but now dilapidated, building, two men were laying some wooden tiles across a wide floor. The guide explained that the hall would eventually be the showcase room of a new museum. He took me into a side room and gestured inside. "This is what was saved."

The offerings were scant: a few paintings, a set of hunting rifles, a royal throne, a group of ornaments and a bookcase and, bizarrely, the skeleton of a large dinosaur. Its tail was squeezed between the wall and a cabinet containing brass goblets. Patrick told me the bones were found somewhere in the north. The oddest item was at the back, almost hidden in shadows. Inside a glass case was a monkey orchestra decked out in fancy frills. Each primate was playing silent violins, violas and drums. Napoleon III had presented it as a gift to Madagascar in the late nineteenth century.

"So who is paying for all this construction and repair?" I asked Patrick.

"The French government, mainly, and some from the World Heritage people. But let me tell you something: most of the money they send is … diverted elsewhere. That is why the repairs are still going on, over twenty years since the fire."

I sighed in recognition. "A pile of cash arrives to repair the Rova, but this man takes his cut, and that man takes his cut, and by the time they've all taken their cut, there's hardly anything left."

"Precisely."

Back outside, I thanked Patrick for his assistance and gave him a 10,000 note as a tip, which was about three dollars. He shook my hand and returned up the hill to the gates of the Rova. As for me, I found my taxi and headed back into the thick of Tana.

6

I asked the driver to stop by Lake Anosy. I wanted to walk back to the hotel before it grew dark. "Keep your camera out of sight," he warned before taking his leave. "Many thieves here."

I nodded and climbed out. In front of me was the Hotel Carlton, maybe a ten-minute walk away. There was a path on my right that led around the edge of the lake, but to get to the actual water's edge I had to cross through a small section of greenery, the favoured resting place for some of the city's residents, either asleep or else sitting in small groups chatting away. A few stalls were selling green apples and watermelons. One chancer spotted me, bounding up with a selection of wooden drums.

"No thanks," I said. The man looked so crestfallen that I almost gave him a few hundred ariary, but the thought of a melee of hawkers hounding my every move made me stick to my guns. Instead, I walked to the edge of the dirty brown and possibly mosquito-ridden lake. In the middle stood a winged woman on a plinth. She was supposedly golden, but if she was, then grime had long since blackened her veneer. Behind the statue was the steep hill that led to the Rova.

"Bonjour. Ça va?" asked a male voice.

It belonged to a wiry man in his early twenties.

"Ça va, très bien," I replied. He asked if I needed a guide. "No thanks," I said in English.

He switched to English, too. "I show you statue. We walk together. Monsieur, you have a nice camera. May I see it?"

I put my camera in my pocket, wrapping a hand tightly around it. My other hand went around my wallet. "Sorry, I'm just leaving."

"Where you from?" He started moving with me.

"England."

"You are here alone?"

I didn't like the way the conversation was going, especially when another young man joined him. I shook my head and told him I was meeting a friend and moved back to the safety of the main road. The men followed me, walking by my side, not saying anything to me, but speaking quietly to each other, as if sizing me up. I doubted I was going to be mugged in broad daylight, but I quickened my pace, nevertheless.

Ahead of me was the Carlton Hotel, and I crossed the road towards it. The men looked like they were going to follow, but stopped and returned to their shadows. My flirtation with Antananarivo's underbelly had ended with nothing apart from me missing some photo opportunities of the lake.

7

Just after I ordered a meal of zebu stew in the hotel restaurant, a large, overly-dressed black woman appeared at my table. She looked to be in her late forties.

"Hi," she said in an American accent. "I'm Lorna. I overheard you speaking to the waiter and when I realised you were a Brit, I just wanted to know whether it would be okay to join you for dinner. I'll pay for my own food, of course. It's just that I don't wanna sit by myself in a restaurant. I don't wanna give people – especially men – the wrong idea. And when I saw your wedding ring, and you tapping away on your laptop thing, I figured you'd be a safe bet."

I was flabbergasted. My mouth opened and then closed. "Of course," I stuttered. "Take a seat."

Lorna turned out to be great company. Over a few glasses of wine (for her) and two bottles of Three Horse Beer (for me), she told me she was from Texas, had been in Antananarivo for two days and had not left the hotel once. "I am too scared. You hear about things. Besides, it looks so ... unclean. I don't know how you can walk around by yourself. You must be so brave."

I smiled bashfully and found out that Lorna was in Madagascar for a very specific reason. The previous year, she had done some research into her family history and had discovered that her great-great-great-great-grandfather (on her mother's side) hailed from the island. "He was a slave, shipped over to Massachusetts in 1719. He was only twenty-three."

Lorna recounted how a Virginia slave owner bought him and made him toil in his tobacco fields, which he did for the next few years. Then he met a female slave and they had a child together. That little girl grew up a slave, but after the American civil war, they were set free. "The daughter moved to Texas where she met a soldier. They ended up having six children, one of whom was my maternal great-grandfather."

I nodded appreciatively at the story. Slaves, a tropical island, tobacco barons and civil war: it sounded like a plotline for a historical novel. I told Lorna this.

"That's what I thought, too. And tomorrow there's a new chapter: a woman is meeting me here in the hotel. She's one of my cousins. I've never met her before, only talked online. Anyway, she's going to take me to meet her husband and children. Part of me is thrilled, but the other half is scared to death. But I had to come here. I just *had* to."

I commended her on her mission and wished her every success and happiness with the outcome. As we shook hands and bade each other farewell, I retired to my room excited about the next day, too. As the darkness outside stole the shadows, thoughts of lemurs and chameleons, slaves and ancestors reverberated around my mind. With them, I retired from another great day in the tropics.

Clockwise from top left: The view from the Carlton Hotel, overlooking Lake Anosy; Antananarivo in all its busy glory; Painted advertisements are everywhere; Meat sellers along the road to the city; the Rova Palace

Chapter 6: Soldiers, the President and the Lemurs of Andasibe

I awoke the next morning groggy but excited. The Three Horse Beers were stampeding around my head. I focussed on my watch. I had one hour before my guide came to pick me up.

Pulling the curtains apart, I looked down at the city. Armed troops were everywhere. A platoon was directly opposite the hotel, large sub-automatic machine guns at the ready. Another battalion was blocking the road. Their action had caused gridlock. About fifty more armed men with red berets had lined up in tight groups to my right, as if awaiting a parade inspection or preparing for a riot.

I blinked my dream away and re-opened my eyes. The soldiers were still there and more were joining them. Movement caught my attention. Five soldiers were on the roof of the building opposite, fanning out at speed. When one reached the edge, he knelt and looked down. I looked too. It seemed as if war was about to break out. I logged onto the hotel's ponderously slow Wi-Fi to find out what was happening.

2

Madagascar is a place that conjures images of cute creatures and animated movies. But I learned that it is also notorious for its riots. They usually accompany elections.

Since independence from France in 1960, riots, bombings, assassinations and military coups have happened left, right and centre. In 2009, the fiercest riot in the country's history broke out in Antananarivo. The population had simply had enough of the president, and the final straw was when he bought himself a private jet. With protesters running amok in the capital, burning down the TV station, looting shops and then killing a policeman, the president fled to South Africa. By the time the riot petered out two months later, 135 people lay dead. One key effect of the riot was that it destroyed the country's burgeoning tourist industry. Holidaymakers did not want to visit a country where they might be shot.

Antananarivo has remained calm since them, and tourists are trickling back. Even so, the British Foreign Office advises visitors that 'the political situation remains fragile' and to 'avoid crowds and political demonstrations.' It goes on to say that 'crime is widespread'. I searched Google for any breaking news stories about the country. Nothing came up.

Quite suddenly, the lights went out and the air-conditioning stopped humming. The power was out. Then the hotel's generators kicked into action, as they had done numerous times already. With the Wi-Fi down for the time being, I looked back outside, seeing even more troops. Behind the military cordons were the citizens of Tana, who appeared to be in good spirits. As far as I could tell, there were no insurgents running rampage or looters burning shops. The lake looked the same as it had yesterday, with people wandering around it as usual. Apart from the great honking snarl of traffic caused by the roadblock, Tana appeared normal. I decided to investigate by going down to ground level.

3

Descending the lift with me was a tall black gentleman wearing an expensive suit. He was speaking into a mobile phone. "Yes, I have heard that Zuma has made the apology," he said, his voice rich with baritone. He was referring to the South African president's recent public apology for misuse of public funds. "I think it will be a good thing for him to step down."

The man turned and nodded at me, continuing to speak about Zuma's issue to whoever was on the other end of the line. When the door opened at lobby level, another man in a suit was waiting. "Good morning, Mr President," the new man said. "The delegates are waiting for you. I trust your stay was pleasant."

"Thank you, it was," I said, then realised he was talking to the gent with the phone.

I looked at the man now identified as a president. He certainly looked like one – impeccably turned out and with a definite aura of power. Whether he was a president of a country, a company or something else entirely, I had no idea, but if he was the president of an African nation, then it explained the troop activity outside.

I loitered in the elevator while the two suited men walked towards the exit doors. Then I stepped into the lobby, searching for anything out of the ordinary, such as men with guns. Activity seemed perfectly normal. It certainly wasn't a hotel gearing up for battle stations, so I headed outside, too. The president and his aide were already gone and so I walked to my right where a soldier was standing with an assault rifle. He was blocking guests from proceeding further along the road.

"Bonjour," I said. He turned around, assessed me as non-threatening and turned back to the road. In front of him, the military parade had grown, bolstered by a few armoured personnel cars.

"Parlez vous Anglais?" I asked the soldier.

"Non." He didn't even turn around.

I wondered whether to take a photo of the soldiers opposite. Some nations were funny about things like that, so I mimed to the soldier whether it would be okay. He shook his head. Feeling peeved, I looked up at the troops on the roof and saw one hoisting some sort of flag or bunting. When I heard the sound of a trumpet, I concluded that there was not a riot going on after all. It sounded like a parade. Satisfied I was not in immediate danger, I went back inside the lobby to wait for my guide.

4

Out of breath, he arrived ten minutes later. His name was Andry, and he explained that he'd had to park the car half a kilometre away. "The traffic is bad," he said, "even by Tana standards. The police have blocked the roads. I had to beg them to let me walk into the hotel."

Andry was about thirty, with a wispy beard and friendly features. Instead of looking African, he appeared to be from South East Asia, perhaps somewhere like Malaysia. I asked him why all the soldiers and police were there.

"I'm not sure. I think maybe some sort of ceremony, or perhaps some important people are coming."

I told him about the man in the lift.

"That explains it. He will be a VIP. Many presidents stay here in the Carlton. When our own president stays, they put out the red carpet."

Instead of walking right, we headed left, passed a line of three flagpoles (which for some unknown reason featured the flags of Madagascar, Mauritius and the former Soviet Republic of Georgia), and walked past some parked cars that formed the edge of the hotel's grounds. Andry spoke to a soldier blocking the path further ahead, and the man nodded, allowing us passage. Beyond the military barrier, the streets of Antananarivo were busy with people – fruit sellers, shoe shiners and the biggest group: people milling about doing nothing. The lake looked as nice as the previous day and, as we walked along the same well-trodden path, I tried to spot my friendly hustlers from the previous day. They were nowhere in sight.

"Keep your belongings in your pocket," warned Andry, who was carrying my small luggage on his head. "A tourist got robbed here last week. His camera, his wallet and his watch – all taken."

I told him about the two men from yesterday.

"Thieves. If you had not put your camera away so quickly, they would have stolen it. And if you had gone with them to the statue, they would have had more friends with them to rob you."

It seemed I'd had a lucky escape.

The air around me smelled of wood smoke, an aroma that persisted until we passed a huge mango stall. Hundreds of green mangos were piled up, with customers sizing them up and down. I was tempted to buy one, but Andry suggested we keep moving. "People are watching us."

Inside the car, Andry locked the door and then asked whether it would be okay for another person to join us on the two-day tour of Andasibe National Park. He explained that she was a young trainee guide, who had never been to the park. "It will be good training for her to see how I interact with you, and to listen to the questions you ask."

I couldn't really refuse; besides, she was already on her way to meet us. Five minutes later, a young woman turned up and introduced herself as Erica. She was twenty-two, pretty and was dressed in western clothes. Like Andry, Erica's features looked more Asian that African. She took a seat in the back and looked hopelessly embarrassed.

5

The streets of Tana, even away from the soldier-blocked centre, were clogged to high heaven, but I didn't mind, for it gave me a chance to observe people up close. They were wandering the shack stores, sitting around under trees or crammed into the back of minibuses. The more affluent ones were riding in ancient Renault taxis. I spotted a mother breastfeeding a baby in a tiny doorway, a man carrying a pair of chickens by their feet, another pulling a cart piled high with bananas and then a zebu cow wandering unabashedly through it all. Everything was vibrant and in your face, chaotic but working.

Some stalls and buildings, I noted, featured colourful advertisements. Instead of poster billboards, someone had painted these by hand. Whoever the artists were, they were good. One was advertising a packet of something called Supreme Noodles. The packaging had been faithfully painted in three dimensions; compete with folds, crinkles and reflections. Even the chicken drumstick looked real.

As the outskirts of the big city fell behind, Madagascar turned into a land of waterlogged paddy fields and verdant terraced hills. We passed villages with names such as Ambohitsitompo, Mandaka and Mandrakandriana, all of them centred upon a high street of busy stalls and cheap eateries. Mandrakandriana featured a railway station too. Some rusty tracks led off into a nearby field.

"The French built the railway," said Andry, noticing me looking. A woman was walking along the tracks with a bundle of sticks balanced on her head. "They built three lines and many stations, but only one line still works. The train runs twice a week. That's why people use the track as pathways."

By now, Erica looked less nervous, but still preferred to keep quiet in the back. All she offered was that she had been working at the tour company for two months, and that before that, she worked in a school.

"As a teacher?" I asked.

She shook her head. "Helper only."

Our road was a simple two-lane highway, and yet it was the only major route that headed east. This meant trucks were using it all the time, spilling diesel and puffing out lung-blackening smoke, but, most of all, hindering our progress. Even worse was when we encountered a broken down truck. The thin road would suddenly shrink, with cars, buses, trucks, zebu cattle, geese and pedestrians all moving onto the dusty verge or else meandering onto the other side of the road. But despite the obstacles, the traffic never stopped moving. Until the police roadblocks.

Andry had already warned me about the police. "They are corrupt, but I can understand why. The government do not pay them much, so they have to make their own money. Road blocks are one way." A policeman was standing in the middle of the road. He watched us approach, but then waved us past. He stopped the truck behind us instead.

"Why didn't he stop us?" I asked.

"I think he saw you. The government does not want them to interfere with tourists. They know that if tourists stop coming to Madagascar, then things will be even worse. That is why that tourist who was mugged last week was big news. If the police find the thieves, they will punish them harshly."

6

Almost two hours after leaving Antananarivo, we arrived at the Peyrieras reptile sanctuary. Originally founded by a French zoologist, for whom it was named, it was now run by his daughter, who was in France at the time of my visit. The small centre was the halfway point of the journey to the national park and, as well as offering a choice selection of Malagasy creatures, it would serve as a lunch stop. But first, a local guide took Erica and me (Andry elected to remain with the car) inside a large meshed enclosure where chameleons of every shade and colour resided. Bright red ones, vivid green ones, big ones, small ones; lizards were everywhere. Almost all of them were perched on branches, their swivelling eyes watching us with great interest and consternation. If we leaned too close, they would open their mouths and glare.

"This one here," said the young man showing us around, "is a Malagasy giant chameleon, the biggest species in the world." Erica and I stared at the large orange and black specimen that was ever-so-slowly tight-roping across a thin branch. It was about a foot long. "This is only a juvenile. It will grow twice the length it is now."

As well as the chameleons, the centre was home to a collection of snakes, lizards and long nosed hedgehogs, but the star attraction was a group of lemurs. After hiking up a hillside trail, clutched by dense forest on both sides, our guide began clicking and whirring, presumably making lemur-inducing noises. Nothing came. He tried again, louder this time. Still, nothing came. He looked a little annoyed.

"Wait here," he told us. "I will go deep into the forest to flush the little bastards out." Actually, he didn't say that, but that's what he was probably thinking. Off he went, crashing through the undergrowth, making his animal noises, leaving Erica and me to shuffle our feet. Then a lemur appeared in a tree next to us. Erica spotted it first. As we stared, the long-tailed, black and ginger monkey-like creature nimbly sprang to another tree like an acrobat. And there it regarded us.

I tried to take a photo just as another lemur appeared, again a cute thing about the size of a dog but with the colours of a panda. Their faces were black but ringed in a band of comically fluffy white fur. Suddenly, the pair began to rip through the canopy, jumping and landing on branches and tree trunks with incredible ease. From tree to tree they leapt, before returning to a branch nearby. Then the guide reappeared; he looked apologetic. "Sorry, I think the lemurs are shy today, or maybe they've been spooked by a snake."

I pointed at the pair over in the trees.

His eyes widened. "Ah, the Sifiku lemurs have found you."

He began to make his noises again, which coaxed one of them closer. It wanted the piece of banana in the guide's hand, eyeing the fruit hungrily. Then it reached over and took the chunk from the guide's outstretched hand.

Up close, the lemur was as delightful as anything. Its fluffy fur looked as soft as a kitten's. The guide passed a chunk of banana to me and the lemur's eyes followed it. Holding my palm out, a foot from the creature's grasp, it hesitated, then – quick as a flash – reached over and grabbed it. Next, it was Erica's turn. She giggled and squealed as it touched her hand. I was glad to be sharing the experience with someone equally as excited. A few minutes later, the lemurs grew bored, especially when the bananas ran out. With the show over, we returned to find Andry.

7

After lunch (zebu steak and rice), the three amigos were back on the road to Andisibe. The landscape was paddy field followed by paddy field. In most of them, people toiled, backs arched, ankles submerged. Sometimes, they would be in canoes, the water so deep that they needed boats to get to the middle. At the edge of these deep-water fields, white egrets stood sentinel, watching over ducks, geese and the occasional zebu cattle.

We passed through another village caressed by gorgeous hills. Andry slowed down. "I need to buy some water," he said. As soon as we came to a standstill, a horde of fruit sellers gathered around the doors. Bananas, papayas, pomegranates, stems of ginger and some small red things that looked like apple hybrids lay on trays, all balanced deftly on the women's upturned palms.

"Please get out and have a look around. It is very safe," Andry told me. "Erica and I will be about ten minutes."

I climbed out and bought a couple of bananas and one of the red things. It tasted sour, like an over-ripe apple. While Andry and Erica went off to buy the water, I took in the village of Ambodiamontana. It resembled a Wild West town, in that everything was spread out along one section of road. Instead of saloons and a sheriff's jailhouse, there were cheap eateries, fruit hawkers, a proliferation of convenience stalls (that mainly sold biscuits) and a small church. A woman walked past me carrying a basket of live chickens on her head. She didn't give me a second glance, and then I realised why. The town was busy with Westerners, most stocking up on provisions before embarking on their long camping trips into the forest. As if to prove this, a minibus pulled up, attracting the immediate attention of the fruit ladies, and from it spilled out some serious-looking adventurers, decked with waterproofs, dangling cans of insect repellent and sturdy boots. I ate one of my bananas and returned to the car where Erica and Andry were already waiting.

"Have you noticed," said Andry, as we headed away from the little but frenzied town, "how some people from Madagascar look like they are from Indonesia and Malaysia?" In front, a truck was making sloth-like headway up one of the many hills that dotted the landscape.

I nodded.

"That's because people from Borneo came here by outrigger canoe in the ninth century—"

"They came to Madagascar by canoe? All the way from Borneo?" It seemed improbable.

"Yes. I know it seems unbelievable that people five thousands kilometres away could settle on this island. But that's what happened. They settled and had children and now they make up almost a quarter of the population. The Merino, one of the eighteen ethnic tribes of Madagascar, can trace their DNA back to just thirty women from Borneo, which explains our Indonesian features. Erica and I are both Merino, and one day I would like to visit Indonesia and see how much I look like the people there."

8

The town of Moramanga lies in a plateau surrounded by highland. Like all the other towns we passed through, its fortune lay in its intersection. Crammed by it, and then spilling off in all four directions were goods shops, repair shacks, mobile phone top-up stalls and gaudily painted hotels. More interestingly, the town has a small, mostly forgotten monument that consists of a concrete tubular structure encased inside a white fence. On all four sides of its square base, plaques read: 29 Marsa 1947.

On the evening of that date, a group of disgruntled local men from Moramanga grabbed spears and whatever else they could find and charged a French police camp near the railway line. By the time the French realised they were under attack, it was already too late: twenty of them were dead. With the camp taken, the men moved on towards other French camps and plantations, as did other groups of armed men in the area. Soon more people joined the cause against French colonial rule, including a million peasants in the south.

The French didn't take this lightly. They quickly assembled a mighty force of soldiers, bolstered from their other African colonies, and stamped down hard on the Malagasy Rebellion. And even though it is hard to imagine French people doing this, they murdered and raped their way through the countryside, burned down villages they suspected of harbouring nationalists and brutally killed any nationalists they found. At one point, they dragged eighteen women to an airstrip, forced them aboard a troop-carrying aircraft and then, at altitude, threw each one out to their death. On another occasion, they gathered 150 men into wagons and machine-gunned the whole lot. This atrocity had taken place not far from where Andry, Erica and I were now driving. By the time the rebellion was over, 30,000 Malagasy were dead. When news of the brutality reached Paris, the French government were so disgusted that they decided to suppress all news about it in the media. They knew that their reputation would be in tatters if things got out. It took until 2005 for any official acceptance by the French of what actually happened.

We stopped the car near the monument. Apart from a few pigeons and a man carrying a large sack across his shoulders, we were the only people there. The base looked like it needed a lick of paint, as did the fence. "There is a mausoleum nearby," said Andry. "Inside it, the remains of thousands of people killed by the French are housed."

"So how did Madagascar gain independence?" I asked. "If the French put down the rebellion so hard, why did they eventually agree to leave?"

Andry shrugged. "A few years later, they relaxed their hold over the country. I think that maybe they were sickened by their own actions. They even allowed a few reforms. By 1960, they handed it over. And that was when everything fell apart – the railways, the building work, the economy. By 1979, Madagascar was bankrupt. Nineteen years of independence and there was nothing in the bank."

9

Almost six hours after leaving Antananarivo, we arrived at the edge of Andasibe National Park. Vast swathes of forest lay in all directions, thick and lustrous: an explosion of branches, stems, leaves and darkened tree trunks. Instead of stopping, we followed a long road that led along one edge, passing a series of hotels built for foreign tourists: most of them lay empty.

My place of stay was the Vakona Forest Lodge, an outpost of relative luxury among the trees. Its central building was on stilts and overlooked a small greenish lake. After I checked in, a hotel employee took me to my own private lodge. It had a ground balcony that offered a view of pure forest; inside, it had an upper bedroom, a study, a small bathroom and plenty of mosquito nets.

I dropped my bag on the bed and returned to the balcony outside. From the depths of the forest came the constant chatter of birds and the cacophony of frog call: the purest sound of the tropics I'd heard so far. Out there, somewhere, were lemurs, and plenty of them. And I was about to see some of them.

I locked my lodge door, avoiding the praying mantis lurking by the keyhole, and went to meet Andry and Erica by the main building. The remainder of the day would be made up of two parts: a visit to Lemur Island, which was part of the lodge complex, and then, when it got dark, a night walk along the edge of the national park. Both prospects excited me.

To get to the tiny lemur island, Erica and I had to sit in a small canoe. Andry waved us goodbye from the water's edge, leaving us in the hands of an experienced lemur guide. The journey to the other side took all of ten seconds and I wondered why the lodge hadn't built a bridge, but the answer was obvious: with a bridge, the lemurs could all escape the island. Instead, they were captive on a lush tropical island, where people like me could see them up close.

And close they indeed were.

Erica was out of the canoe first, her mobile phone's camera pointing to a huddle of six or seven brown lemurs, smaller than the black and white ones we had seen earlier, which were jumping around in some nearby grass. I climbed out next, closely followed by the guide.

Lemurs were everywhere and all of them were friendly. One sauntered up to our guide, wanting a piece of fruit from his hand. It was so close that I crouched to stroke its thick fur. It felt like a cat. As I did so, another jumped on my shoulder, sitting there while the guide took a photo.

"These are common brown lemurs," the guide told us. "And that one there is a black and white lemur." The newcomer was similar to the ones we had seen in the reptile sanctuary, except it was far cuter and had the brightest orange eyes I'd seen in any animal. His main pastime was wanting to fight the smaller brown ones. It reared up on its hind legs and screeched at the one closest to it. Its little cousin scarpered. Erica laughed and so did I. The black and white lemur then stretched out into the grass, lying flat on its back. The white tufts on the side of its head made it look like a clown. We left him to it and wandered further inland.

Lemur Island was even smaller that I had first thought and, in less than thirty seconds, we had walked to the other side. Beyond the water was more jungle, busy with lemurs leaping, hanging upside down and generally playing for tourists with cameras. We caught another canoe across and met up with an Australian couple in their seventies.

"This is amazing," the white-haired gent said. "These animals are amazing."

His wife didn't say anything, casting a glance from me to Erica and then back to me. Just then, a terrific crashing made us all look upwards. There, in the canopy, a large ginger-coloured lemur was performing some death-defying acrobatics. First, it swung around on one hand, then, after screeching like a banshee, it catapulted – Tarzan-like – from one branch to the next. And then it was gone, its calls cascading around the forest. With its departure, we too took our leave.

10

That evening, Andry drove Erica and me along a pitch black road, where everything beyond the scope of the headlights was pure darkness. Eventually we stopped beside what I took to be an abandoned railway office. Instead of being murdered, I was introduced to Edward, an experienced night-time forest guide. Edward had a torch strapped to his forehead, which he pointed through Andry's window. In our startled state, we all shook hands and then Erica and I climbed out, leaving Andry to stay with the car.

Edward was in his mid-forties and had worked most of his adult life as an Andisibe guide. "I studied botany at university," he told us, "and I am an expert in trees and plants, even ferns. I can recognise every species of plant indigenous to Madagascar."

We began a walk along a quiet stretch of road bereft of artificial light. Because of this, the stars above us were mesmerising. I could not recall a time in my life when I had seen so many dots of astral light. I gazed at them, dazzled by the white sparkles, clustered nebula and distant galaxies. As I did so, the calls of a thousand tree frogs and the powerful aroma of the unseen blooms filled the air.

As well as the torch on his head, Edwards had a more powerful one in his hand. He started skimming them both in the trees, searching for any tell-tale reflections from lemurs' eyes. A few metres further, he stopped. "Woolly lemur," he said, shining his hand torch up into a patch of blackness. How he'd noticed the eyes was beyond me, but with the more powerful beam staying still, I could indeed see a pair of orange dots in the blackness.

I asked how he could tell it was a woolly lemur.

"Big eyes. Woolly lemurs have the biggest eyes of all the lemurs."

As we watched, they blinked off. The lemur had either moved or turned its back on us.

A few hundred yards further, Edward spotted another pair of eyes. The two distant, but eerily bright, eyes looked the same as the others, but Edward said they belonged to a common brown lemur.

Before I could ask how he knew, he said, "Different colour."

The only explanation was that Edward possessed superhuman eyes, and later, even though his head light barely skipped over the surface of some nearby bushes, he saw a chameleon. Substituting its bright daytime colour scheme, the lizard was a dull whitish-grey, which Edward explained was how all chameleons looked at night. This one, with its face full of light, looked annoyed; its bulbous eyes swivelled in alarm.

"Are there any dangerous animals in Madagascar?" I asked.

"Only crocodiles over in the west. And some scorpions that can sting a little, but that's it."

"No snakes or spiders?"

"We have many snakes and spiders, but none that are poisonous."

On the way back to meet Andry, Edward found a tree frog. The tiny green amphibian was sitting on a leaf trumpeting out a call for a mate. Its chest bulged and then retracted. The beam of light shining its way didn't bother it one little bit. I took a photo, the only one that turned out okay on the entire walk. Then we retraced our steps back to the start of the road.

11

The next morning, I was up early for my three-hour walk inside Andasibe National Park. It was a twenty-minute drive away from the Vakona Lodge and Edward, the man from the previous evening, was to be my and Erica's guide again.

The forest walk took us along a well-trodden path that cut through dense rainforest. Towering trees, thick foliage and rapid birdcall signalled our every move. As well as the three of us, the jungle was awash with other tourists, all under the expert care of their individual guides. Sometimes we'd cross paths or, more often, hear them somewhere ahead of us. Each guide knew how to make lemur sounds and worked in unison to entice them down. If one guide found a lemur, he would call the others so that there could be as many as twenty people huddled underneath the canopy. This is where I experienced something uncomfortable and quite unexpected. It was because of Erica, though not her fault by any means.

It was probably because she was dressed in Western clothes, young and pretty, and taking photos along with the rest of us. With her Indonesian features, a lot of people assumed she was my wife, especially with the wedding ring on my finger. I caught a disapproving glance from one Western woman in her forties. Her eyes flicked from Erica to me, and she shook her head. The Australian woman had given the same look the previous day. Another woman gave me such a disapproving look that I almost shrivelled up there and then. And the thing was, there was nothing I could do about it except take their judgement. After all, I fitted the bill perfectly in their eyes: a middle-aged letch with a young Asian woman in tow, flaunting her like some trophy.

Now, of course, this could have been in my head. The looks might have been for something else entirely – like maybe I had forgotten to pull up my flies, or maybe I had a splash of ketchup on my chin, but I didn't think so. At least I now knew I could never have a Thai bride; I simply could not take the looks from other people.

Edward, Erica and I moved off by ourselves, and I calmed down. Then there was the call from another guide to our left, and we rushed over to join the throng. Once more, I caught the looks of the assembled Western tourists and so, while everyone began to coo underneath a family of three ginger lemurs, I tried to distance myself from Erica, moving to a clearing a bit further away. Like a dutiful South Asian bride, she followed me through the foliage, shadowing my every move, even brushing my shoulder when a rain of leaves landed on it. Resigned to my fate, I manoeuvred past three young men from Sweden, who eyed Erica up, and felt like shouting through the forest that Erica was not my wife and was in fact a trainee guide. But what would be the point?

As we passed through a deep and dark thicket, free of judgemental Western tourists, I decided to test Edward on his plant identification skills. I pointed at a green plant that to me looked the same as all the others around it.

"It is a bird's nest fern. The Latin name is *Asplenium nidus*."

I pointed at a small plant with a profusion of bright blue berries. It looked quite beautiful and Edward gave me the name in English and in Latin, neither of which I caught. "It is related to coffee plant," he said.

As well as his plant identification prowess, Edward was also an astute birdwatcher. I lost count of the times he pointed at a distant branch and identified the tiny shape fluttering around the leaves. One I did see: the paradise flycatcher. It was a long-tailed bird with a blue head and vivid red body. When it flew away, possibly startled by a falling leaf, Edward told us he was famous in Malagasy ornithological circles. He had once discovered a new species of Indonesian finch while out on a trek in the northern part of the country. "I was very proud," he told us, puffing out his chest like a tree frog. "But that was long time ago now."

Three hours later, the walk was over and, despite the looks I'd received from certain people, I had enjoyed myself. We had seen the largest species of lemur, the Indri (a black and white creature that could make a horrific screeching sound if it so wanted – which it did, often) and had rushed through rainforest trails and ambled along tropical rivers. I thanked Edward for showing it all to us and gave him a large tip to supplement his salary as an official guide. It was time to leave Andasibe and drive back to Tana.

12

The long drive back took us through the same landscape of paddy fields, distant hills and occasional, but busy, towns. As we approached the capital, with dusk fast approaching, fruit bats skimmed over the road, looking like mini pterodactyls. Stuck in a line of traffic, I asked Andry about corruption in his country.

"It is bad. People have to pay bribes all the time, especially to the police and government. Madagascar needs a strong president who is prepared to say no. During elections, they all promise that they will say no to corruption, but when they get into power, they do not change a thing. But it is hard for them. Everyone underneath, from the office boy to the vice-president, is taking their cut, and if a president wants to stop it, they have to fight them all."

I saw a woman limp by, clearly struggling to walk. She looked rake thin, shuffling past a row of soup shacks. "What about people like her?" I asked. "Does the government look after her if she is ill or loses her job?"

Andry shook his head. "They are on their own. Take my parents: they both lived in a nice suburb of Tana, raising my two sisters and me. They sent us to school every day so we could get a good education. My father worked in a printing press for many years. Then it burned down and he lost his job. Luckily, he found a job in the ex-president's milk factory. But then, during the riots of 2009, this factory burned down and my father didn't have a job again. By this time, he was an old man and could not find anywhere else to work. Luckily, we were all grown up so he didn't have to worry about us. Other families were not so lucky. Anyway, after a short while, he and my mother left Tana for the countryside. They're still there now, growing their own food and living a simple life by the river."

It sounded nice, idyllic even. "Are they happy?"

"That is a good question. They are happy because they are safe and know their children are doing well, but I know my father finds it hard to accept things. Remember, he was once a man of means in the city, a man held in high regard by his neighbours and friends, and yet he is now just a simple farmer."

By the time Andry and Erica dropped me off at a hotel near the airport, it was pitch black. I thanked them both, especially Andry. He had been a great guide: friendly, open and full of good advice. Erica too deserved thanks. She had helped me get some good photos of lemurs, plus it was nice to share the experience of the playful creatures with her, even if she was only my pretend wife.

I retired to my room weary but fulfilled. Madagascar had promised much but delivered more.

Clockwise from top left: A tree frog from the night walk; fruit-selling women of Ambodiamontana; me with a friendly lemur; Chameleons are great; Andry and Erica – great guides; Lemurs are impossibly cute

Chapter 7: Windhoek: meteorites and dassies

From Madagascar, I flew westwards, stopping briefly in Johannesburg before boarding a second South African Airways flight to Windhoek (pronounced Vind-hook), capital of Namibia. Aboard this second flight were two Tanzanian diplomats, a man and a woman both in their forties. They were sitting in my row.

I could not miss this opportunity. Surreptitiously allowing my pen to fall into the woman's lap, I immediately apologised and then introduced myself. After a few moments, I ascertained two things: they were a husband and wife diplomatic team from Dar es Salaam and they were on their way to Windhoek for some kind of meeting. They didn't elaborate on the meeting and, instead, told me about Tanzania, principally how nice both Zanzibar and the Serengeti National Park were. I listened, nodding in the right places, but all the while really wanting to ask about their diplomatic privileges. In particular, I wanted to know about diplomatic pouches. I'd read that Western diplomats, flying into the likes of Saudi Arabia, often smuggled bottles of whisky inside their diplomatic bags, knowing they would be immune to prying eyes. Finally, during a lull in the conversation, I went straight out and asked the woman whether she ever carried one.

"Sometimes," she said. The woman reminded me of Dusty Lee, a TV cook from my youth. "Why do you ask?" She suddenly looked suspicious. Her husband studied me, too.

I smiled disarmingly in case they thought I was some sort of thief. "I've always wondered about them, that's all. I read somewhere that you can put whatever you like in them, all under the cloak of diplomatic immunity, and that security won't ever check them. I just want to know whether this is true."

My answer calmed her. Her husband answered my query. "Yes, our bags sometimes have diplomatic clearance, but I have never taken anything I shouldn't into another country, if that's what you're asking. Neither has my wife."

I nodded, praising them for their honest ways, secretly disappointed they were not smuggling diamonds into Namibia. Or maybe they were and weren't saying.

2

Namibia is one of Africa's success stories. Prior to the 1800s, bushmen and nomadic herders were the only people who dotted the desert and arid landscape of Namibia. No one in Europe even cared. But then someone discovered vast hordes of diamonds, and things changed. In the blink of an eye, the Germans arrived, grabbed the diamond mines and renamed the land German South-West Africa. And this is how things stayed for a while, right up until the Germans' defeat at the end of World War I.

With the Germans packing up, South Africa stepped in to fill the void. White South Africans poured in, securing the most lucrative and important jobs and setting up their homes and farms in the best locations. Things turned worse when South Africa's infamous apartheid policy came into play across the country in 1948. As in South Africa, blacks and whites were segregated, blacks forcibly removed from their homes to live in their own areas, made to sunbathe on their own beaches and rest their weary limbs on 'black-only' benches as they made their way to their segregated schools and universities.

After independence from South Africa in 1990, Namibia could have gone one of two ways. The first was to allow its leadership to enjoy unparalleled power, to embrace corruption and to let the rich line their pockets at the expense of its citizens. This was how it usually went for newly independent African nations. The other way was more difficult, because it involved open and democratic elections, a crackdown on backhanders and a reduction in red tape. Namibia chose the latter, using its income from diamonds and precious metal mining operations to revitalise the economy. Instead of politicians taking their cuts, the government poured money into hospitals, education and housing. It built new roads, cleaned up its cities and planted plenty of trees. It also kept in with its larger neighbour, pegged its currency to the South African rand and traded heavily with its old sparring partner. By 2013, Namibia was considered the best emerging market in the African continent. Today, it enjoys one of the highest GDPs in Africa, and compares well with the GDPs of countries such as Indonesia, Bosnia and Jordan. And even better for me was that I didn't need a visa to get into the country, a rarity in Africa these days.

3

Two hours after taking off from Johannesburg, we touched down at Windhoek's Hosea Kutako International Airport. At the gate, I said goodbye to the diplomats, rushed down the steps and legged it across the tarmac. I was the third person to reach immigration, but before I could get to the booth, a woman held out her hand. "Stand on the line and look into the camera."

I stopped, noticing my image appearing on a screen. As in Nairobi, it was a temperature check for Ebola. I passed muster, and she waved me past; my cold had departed in Madagascar somewhere, thankfully. The immigration counters in front were still free, and I bagged one, thrusting my passport under the little gap in the Perspex. A minute later, a kind-faced woman stamped me into Namibia; it was less than fifteen minutes since touchdown. This is what Africa can do, I thought, when unnecessary bureaucracy is cleared from the system. Namibia's immigration systems were working like clockwork. Just this little thing had put me into a good mood and I hoped the Tanzanian diplomats took note. I spotted them heading towards their own special immigration booth.

Before I left the airport, I changed some US dollars into Namibian dollars, pleased that the exchange was massively in my favour. The Namibian dollar was pegged at the same rate as the South African rand, which meant their currencies peaked and dropped together. Ever since turmoil in the Chinese markets (a major export partner with South Africa), coupled with slow economic growth across the border, both currencies had almost halved in value. I bought a can of Diet Coke, and instead of costing me 80p as it had before, it was now only 45p. I jumped in a taxi and gave the driver the hotel address.

The driver was a young man who tutted every time someone overtook him. When a black 4x4 charged past us on the brow of a blind hill, he actually swore. "That maniac could've killed us if a truck had been coming the other way! We would both be dead right now. Idiot!"

Outside, the countryside looked distinctly African: an endless savannah-like expanse that ended at a range of distant mountains. Just beyond the highway, on both sides, ran a parallel metal fence, presumably to keep dangerous wildlife off the road. It looked like prime cheetah habitat to me and I asked the driver whether the large cats were found in Namibia.

"Yes, cheetahs are around here. If you visit a game reserve, you will see. Is that why you're here?"

I told him my well-versed story, that I was just a tourist visiting some friends in the capital. This was the best way of fending off unwanted offers of tours. The driver accepted this and resumed his driving at the posted speed limit, the only driver doing so, apart from lumbering trucks.

"Shit!" yelped the driver. He had been about to overtake one large truck when we heard the massive, elongated beep. We swung back in behind the truck as another maniac in a 4x4 thundered past at a ridiculous speed. Like the earlier madman, he was a middle-aged white man.

Most whites in Namibia are Afrikaners, descendants of the old German colonialists. Even after apartheid, they still own around fifty percent of the country's farmland. The man in the 4x4 was probably speeding back to his cattle ranch.

When my taxi driver had calmed down, I asked him whether he'd ever been to South Africa. He nodded. "Many times. I can drive passengers to Cape Two in two days, with a night of rest in between. The border crossing is easy and takes no time at all. That's because South African border officials are friendly. Not like the Botswana and Angolan border guards. They are always in a bad mood. The only thing that makes them happy is a bribe."

"So there's no corruption in Namibia?"

"Of course there is! This is Africa, there will always be corruption. But it is not as bad as other places. Mainly it's politicians doing deals or giving favours to their family. Nothing major."

4

Twenty minutes later, we hit the outskirts of Windhoek, home to around 400,000 people. We passed a large school that was churning out teenage girls, all wearing white blouses and green pleated skirts. The children were a mixture of races, but mainly blacks. The street they were spilling out onto looked well ordered and clean, a world away from the streets of Djibouti City and Antananarivo. In fact, Windhoek could've been somewhere in Europe, for it was a city of shiny bank buildings, modern shopping malls and billboards advertising the best rates for mobile phone data.

I noticed a gated community surrounded by barbed wire and electric fences. It was protecting large homely villas. Further on, we passed another gated community, the barbed wire uglifying the whole street it adjoined. The presence of security cameras, metal fences and strips of wire that would electrocute a person were ominous signs that, for all its show of wealth and prosperity, there was an underlying threat of crime. In fact, Namibia, like its neighbour, had one of the highest murder rates in the world, most of them occurring in Windhoek.

Namibians also kill their children. Every year, tiny babies are found at the bottom of rivers or stuffed into garbage bins. Other newborns are buried in waste ground or thrown into sewers. A few years ago, a large water company in Windhoek claimed they were finding a dozen dead babies in their sewerage systems every month. And the babies had been cut into small pieces so they could be flushed down toilets. Who does this and why would a person do such a thing? Well, the reasons are complex, but usually involve young women who fear their family will shun them if they find out they are with baby. Or it might be the case that a single mother will not be able to work if she has a baby in tow, so her choice is stark: keep the baby and starve or kill the baby and live. Others are schoolgirls who cannot face the backlash they will undoubtedly receive from their parents, classmates and teachers; some are prostitutes or women in affairs. Baby killing is a growing problem in Namibia.

As well as murders and infanticides, Namibia (and, in particular, Windhoek) is a hotbed of assaults, robberies, carjacking and burglaries. According to the British Foreign Office, 'Muggers in Windhoek often target foreign tourists ... even in busy city centre locations in broad daylight.' With thoughts of mayhem running though my consciousness, the taxi turned right onto Independence Avenue, one of the main drags of the city. Palm trees, car showrooms, safari tourist agencies and craft shops all vied for attention along the darkening street. Before I had a chance to take it all in, we pulled up outside my hotel.

5

The next morning, I was ambling along Independence Avenue in full view of potential muggers. From my extensive travels, I had discovered that government travel advice was something to be heeded, but not dwelt upon. It was the government's job to inform people, and this they did with clinical caution. But here, in situ, with the sun shining down on the street, I felt about as safe as anywhere.

It was hot, though, and promised to be even hotter later on. I pulled my cap tighter and wandered by a craft bazaar. A single line of stalls made up the market, most of them selling the same things: wooden carvings, cloth and trinkets. The naked women were unusual, though. At some of the stalls, a bare-breasted woman sat, sometimes with a baby, sometimes not, but always proudly displaying her wares. I dared a glance and was rewarded with an outstretched trinket. I shook my head and walked on.

Independence Avenue was full with pedestrians and traffic. The buildings were clean and well kept, though largely nondescript. The pavement I was walking along was in good order and the people around me looked to have a purpose to their steps, rather than just wanting to hang around for potential victims. There were also plenty of white faces heading into banks, sitting in street cafes or simply wandering along. Windhoek, at least so far, was a world away from many African cities I'd visited. Like Port Louis in Mauritius, it was Africa-*lite*.

I entered a small shopping mall, finding it the same as any other in the western world. An optician, a Wimpy bar, a frozen yoghurt shop and a large supermarket vied for space among the clothes and ornament stores. Through the other side, I found something far more interesting nestled between some curio stalls. It was a monument of meteorites.

Four billion years ago, a massive lump of space rock hurtled to Earth, hitting the atmosphere at such speed that the lump fragmented into pieces. These segments rained down upon the prehistoric landscape of Namibia, covering a rough oval-shaped area that was 170 miles long and 60 miles wide. It was (and still is) the biggest meteorite shower the planet has even seen, even though no people ever saw it because, at that point in time, the Earth could not sustain life. Eventually, though, a British explorer, visiting the region in the mid-nineteenth century, noticed that some locals had made spearheads from a suspiciously *spacey* kind of rock. He collected a few samples and, when he returned to England, sent them for testing. The results proved what the explorer thought: they were meteorites.

Since this discovery, most of the Namibian meteorites have been illegally shipped overseas, ending up in the hands of private dealers. Of the remainder, most have been lost, stolen or simply misplaced. By the time the Namibian authorities stepped in, only around thirty individual pieces were left. They collected them up and decided to make a monument. Instead of placing the finished article in a museum, they put it at the crossroads of two busy, pedestrian-only shopping streets. Just across from me was a Specsavers, a Big Baddy fashion store and a Standard Bank building.

I was the only person looking at the monument. Each brown, and vaguely metallic-looking, meteorite stood on its own silver plinth. Some were large, about the size of my head, some smaller, maybe about the size of my foot. Three plinths stood empty; someone had stolen the meteorites intended for them during the monument's construction. I took a photo and then made my way back into the mall to buy a sandwich.

6

With hunger staved off for the time being, I walked back to Independence Avenue, avoiding the religious groups standing around with printed pamphlets and disarming smiles. I'd noticed a lot of them in Windhoek in my short time in the city, all of them young white men. They didn't seem to be getting much interest from the many passers-by.

I found a row of colonial buildings that were quite possibly the only remaining examples of German-built townhouses in the city centre. One of them, the Erkrathus Building, dated from 1910 and looked like it belonged in Munich. Its deliciously sloping red roof and ornate windows made it seem at odds with the other buildings along the busy street, even though it was a department shop. I walked by the Ministry of Justice, and then passed the Hungry Lion fast food joint whose speciality was the Pride Burger. Then, when I reached a large Shoprite store, always a feature in Southern African towns and cities, I retraced my steps and turned uphill. At the top of the slope was Robert Mugabe Avenue, a leafy thoroughfare that ran parallel to Independence Avenue. On one corner was the most famous landmark of Windhoek: Christuskirche.

Christuskirche is a German-built church of beige sandstone and red roof tiles. Even though it was over a century old, it looked as if builders had only finished it the previous week. It was so pristine that it could have been in Denmark or in a fairy tale park. Built during the time of German colonialism, there were no signs of grime, crumbling brickwork or even of a flower out of place in the surrounding garden. A group of workmen were slumbering under the shade of a tree and, when they heard me approach, two of them attempted to jump up. They stopped themselves when they realised I was only a tourist instead of their boss.

Across the road from the church was a huge monument. A massive bronze statue of a man called Sam Nujoma, a Namibian revolutionary hero, stood at the top of some wide steps. Beyond him was a huge shiny gold and black skyscraper standing on four gigantic stilts. It was the Namibian Independence Museum. A few bored-looking security officials sat by the entrance: three women and one man. The man was so bored that he was actually asleep. I asked one of the women whether I could go in and she nodded.

"How much is it?" I inquired.

"There is no entry charge." The man opened an eye slightly, focussed on me briefly and then went back to sleep.

Windhoek moved up another notch in my estimation: a museum for free! I pressed the button for the elevator and went straight to the top floor. Once there, a security guard ushered me back down. "Not allowed. Go down to floor five." I did, and, for the next half an hour or so, I found myself wandering around a tank, a jeep, lots of military clothing and huge panoramic paintings depicting warfare and atrocities.

One particularly gruesome scene caught my eye. It was full of tortured faces and screaming mothers clutching infants, while death and destruction was wrought around them. Its title said: The Cassinga Massacre, 4th May 1978.

On that particular day, South African planes and paratroopers decided to attack a military installation belonging to the People's Liberation Army of Namibia. South Africa claimed the group were insurgents, hostile to South African rule. In particular, they were getting sick of them staging guerrilla attacks. And so, in the early hours of 4 May, an aerial formation of attack aircraft began gathering in the sky. Then, at two minutes past eight in the morning, the first bombs dropped on the Namibian camp, closely followed by helicopters and jets doing strafing runs. Soon after, airborne troops landed, and it wasn't yet nine in the morning. By six in the evening, six hundred Namibians were dead, including 167 women and 298 children. The South African claimed the attack was a key military victory; the Namibians claimed it was a war crime, saying that the camp had been the home of refugees. Regardless, the outcome was devastating for South Africa's international standing. The Cassinga Massacre set in motion a Namibian nationalistic movement, which culminated in independence twelve years later.

7

I was walking back along Robert Mugabe Avenue when I noticed a grand building set back in an expansive garden. It featured high verandas, stately white columns and flagpoles, all flanked by statues and palm trees. It looked like a palace or governmental building, which made me look for guards. There were none that I could see and so, in the absence of a wall or gate blocking my path, I entered the grounds.

A large sign told me it was the Parliament Building of Namibia, and warned me against skateboarding, littering, picking flowers and swimming, but apart from that, I was free to wander. I followed a well-kept pathway that led me through a foliage-covered trestle framework. Out the other side, a pair of long-tailed birds fluttered from a nearby bush, startled by my presence. I carried on walking, occasionally spying the long building in front of me. A few men in suits were standing on a lower veranda, one speaking into a phone. Wondering whether one was the president, I took a photo just as a voice surprised me. I spun to see a security guard. He was speaking into his walkie-talkie thing, but said hello as he walked past me. I watched him climb some sweeping steps towards the parliament building. How refreshing, I thought, to not be told off or screamed at for taking a photo.

Instead of following the guard, I stopped by a high wall to the right of the steps. It was home to a collection of brightly-coloured rock agomas, lizards common to Namibia. They scuttled around at my approach and then, after stopping at a safe distance, raised their orange heads up and down like heavy metal headbangers. One agoma flicked its tongue and captured an ant, which reminded me of my returning hunger. It was lunchtime and so I retreated to the hotel.

8

Over lunch, I started reading the *Namibian Sun*, which ran with the tagline: *Tells it all*. The newspaper's main feature was a story about the jobless youth of Namibia finally getting the chance of employment under a new government scheme. Young, out-of-work Namibians could attend government-sponsored training centres and learn skills enabling them to find work. The article went on to explain that, despite the government's best efforts at providing a corruption-free working environment, over a quarter of the working population were without work, most of them blacks. The figure rose alarmingly for young people under 24. Half of them were unemployed.

I turned a few pages and found the classified section. Instead of cars and washing machines for sale, it was the domain of traditional 'doctors'. One 'practitioner' called Prince Solomon, offered 'Love Spells (for all relationship issues)' claiming he could solve any ailment, including those that affected a person's manhood. He claimed his 'enlargement sperm booster' was best for this.

Full of prime Namibian steak (at a ridiculously cheap price), I headed uphill, passing Windhoek High School. Uniformed children were dribbling out, most of them white kids heading towards large and modern 4x4s. I carried on around a hillside road, leaving the bustle of the city below me. Then I spotted something in the middle of road. It looked like a large rock. As I approached, I squinted, wondering what sort of idiot would manhandle a rock that big and leave it in the centre of a road. If a car came around the corner at speed, it would crash right into it.

But it wasn't a rock – it was a beast! I stopped, and regarded it. The creature looked like an oversized guinea pig crossed with a generous portion of rat. Wondering whether it was dangerous, I considered turning back but, just at that moment, a taxi trundled around the bend and beeped. With that, the thing bounded off into the bushes.

I carried on walking, keeping a sharp eye out for things in bushes. My destination was the botanical garden, which was just along the stretch of road. By the time I reached it, I was sweating and hot. The sun stung my eyes and I wished I'd bought a cheap pair of sunglasses in Mauritius when I'd had the chance. Even worse was when I discovered that the gates of the garden were locked and secure. Cursing myself for not checking whether it was open before setting off, I resigned myself to a long walk back. A car pulling up by the gates stopped me in my tracks. A woman stepped out. "You timed that well," she said. "I've just finished my lunch break."

After the woman let me in, she gave me a map. I mentioned the animal I'd seen in the road.

"Ah, you saw a dassie, a rock hyrax." She pointed to the map. It had a drawing of one in the corner. It looked exactly like the creature I had seen. "You will see them in the park if you tread quietly."

"Are they a type of rat?"

"No, they're related to elephants, actually. They have large incisors."

"Elephants? Wow. Are they dangerous?"

The woman laughed. "Not unless you're a plant. They are very timid."

I thanked the woman and entered the botanical garden.

9

Once more, I found myself the only visitor to a Namibian attraction. In fact, the only other tourists I'd seen had been in downtown Windhoek: a couple of Japanese women were taking photos in Zoo Park, an area of greenery beside the Independence Avenue.

I found some steps that led me to the start of the expansive garden, which was, essentially, a huge closed-off area of Namibian countryside. An electric fence surrounded the entire thing, keeping animals in and humans out. Many of the plants and cacti were labelled and clearly well cared for, and as I wandered around them, I tried to keep my footsteps soft, in case I should encounter a rock hyrax. After half an hour, I deduced they were either in a different place or they had ears like radar dishes. But I came across plenty of lizards, birds and strange chicken-like things that clucked and flapped their wings whenever I came too close. There were also multitudes of flies. They buzzed my ears like tiny helicopters, landing on my hat, my nose and my face. I wafted them away, but they resolutely returned with every step.

And then I saw a hyrax. It was sitting upright on a log about a hundred metres away. It seemed to be sniffing the air. I stood motionless and wondered how to proceed. The track was rough and made of rocks, and I would make a racket if I moved, but the undergrowth to the side was thorny and perhaps home to snakes. I decided to inch forward a step, waiting for the creature to dart. When it didn't, I gingerly took another step, and then another, fully expecting the rock hyrax to make a dash for it. Half way there, I stopped and got my camera out. I zoomed in, but the image was too grainy to make out. And so, for the next five minutes, I crept as silently as I could, wondering why the animal had not moved. Maybe it was rabid, I thought, waiting to sink its massive teeth into my skin. If it wanted to, it could bite by hand off. But then I realised why it hadn't moved: the hyrax was an upturned stub on a fallen tree branch. David Attenborough I was not.

I found a trail that led downhill past a series of large residential properties. Lizards darted across sun-bleached walls, or scurried under parked cars and speedboats. So this is where the rich of Windhoek lived, I realised, gazing into some windows, but seeing nobody there. Ahead of me on a hill, way past the boundary fence, were more large dwellings. Each of them had its own plot of lush land surrounded by horrible barbed wire.

At the bottom of the trail was a pile of bricks. On the pile sat a small rock hyrax. It was definitely a hyrax because as soon as it noticed me, it was gone. I crept up to the brick pile and peered at where the animal had been sitting. There was a gap between the bricks and the wall. This black, lightless gap was the dassie's hiding place. I stepped back and crouched behind a bush.

A minute later, a head popped up. I kept still and waited, whiskers twitching. The rock hyrax looked this way and that, and then, after deciding the giant human had gone, it climbed out fully and relaxed in the sun. And then another one appeared, and then another. Later, I learned that rock hyraxes lived in colonies of up to eighty individuals. I dared raise my camera and a head swivelled in my direction. I managed to snap a photo before they ran for it.

Pleased with myself, I followed the trail back to the entrance, just as some spots of rain began to fall. It made my mind up: I flagged down a taxi and went back to the hotel. Later that night, over another zebu steak and Windhoek Beer, a terrific storm began, full of frightening lightning and terrible crashes of thunder. The windows were like rivers and there was no way I was going outside. Up in my room, as the rain lashed against my window, I realised that I'd rather enjoyed myself in Namibia. Not once had I felt unsafe or in danger of being mugged. Perhaps that would change tomorrow, though, because I was heading into Africa's fourth most dangerous city: Johannesburg.

*Clockwise from top left: Christuskirche, a German-built church;
Robert Mugabe Avenue is quite nice; rock agomas, lizards common
to Namibia; Namibian Independence Museum; A rock hyrax,
otherwise known as a dassie; Meteorites in the middle of the city*

Chapter 8: A brief stopover in Johannesburg or was it the Bronx?

Horrific Murder in Bredasdorp, the grisly headline read. According to the article in the newspaper, an unnamed person found the 23-year old woman, raped and murdered on a building site. Her attacker had bound the young woman's hands, pounded her head with a brick, slit her stomach open and then, when he had finished with her, had thrust a beer bottle into her vagina. She was the mother of a new baby. As horrific as the story was, the police's response was perhaps more shocking. The local commander, responding to the crime, simply stated that the level of brutality against females in the area was 'concerning'.

I shook my head as I read the headline underneath. *Kulis River Mom Brutally Slain*. Across from it was another equally grisly headline: *Alleged Killer was 'Possessed'*. And these were just three headlines on a random day in South Africa, where forty to fifty murders per day was seen as the norm, where 180 women and girls are raped before the stroke of midnight, where human life was worth less than a wallet or a bag of white powder. There was no getting away from it: South Africa was *dangerous*. And yet, despite the horror and perceived peril, I was looking forward to visiting Johannesburg, South Africa's biggest city. I'd transited through it plenty of times in the past – en route to places such as Cape Town, Victoria Falls and Dubai – but I'd never once seen it up close.

With just hand luggage, I cleared the O.R. Tambo Airport in record time, and was sitting in the back of a taxi heading downtown. The sky was gunmetal grey, threatening rain or perhaps something more sinister. On the radio, a rap song called *The Devil is a Lie* blasted out. To me it sounded like *The Devil is Alive*. The driver, a young man who spoke very little, liked it. He turned it up when the chorus began. I looked outside. In the distance, the skyline of Johannesburg stood on the horizon, a panorama of tall skyscrapers and spindly TV towers.

2

Johannesburg is home to almost four million people. Half the population are black, with a quarter white and the rest of mixed race or Asian heritage. Rather similar to Namibia, four in ten people in Johannesburg are unemployed. However, if just looking at the black population, this number rises to nine out of ten. Without a job, and without the prospect of getting one, many turn to crime. It's the only way they can survive.

My taxi stopped at some traffic lights. A man with painted white stripes across his face wanted to wash our windscreen. The taxi driver waved him away in annoyance, and then we passed through a suburb of Johannesburg called Bruma. Adjoining both sides of the road were nice townhouses, all of them protected by barbed wire, electric fences and tall metal gates topped with jagged glass. Then we reached the city proper, where shops guarded by heavy-duty steel bars seemed the order of the day. Behind the shops were decaying tower blocks, each one more dirtied and broken than the last. A man with a large satellite dish across his shoulders was walking with another man carrying a large white sack filled with something lumpy. Both looked furtive, or was it my imagination? Across from them, a huddle of young men loitered outside a dingy car repair shop called Biafra Tyres. Graffiti was everywhere, as were piles of rubbish. It was as if I was driving through the set of a 1970s cop movie from the Bronx. And then, in the midst of all this despair, we pulled up outside the hotel.

3

My room was on the seventeenth floor and afforded a grand view of Johannesburg. High-rise office blocks, tall bank buildings and a large train station took up much of what I could see. It reminded me a little of New York, albeit a broken version. What had clearly been a well groomed city was now broken and filthy, under siege from its inhabitants who cared not a jot for its care. And yet, as I was soon to discover, the view from my hotel window was the best it would get.

Before venturing onto the mean streets of Jo'burg, I went to the very top of the hotel where I found a small bar. As the only patron, I bought a bottle of Castle Beer to steady my nerves and got chatting to the barman. I wanted to know about places I could visit.

"You want to leave the hotel?" He looked concerned.

I nodded. "Just to take a few photos."

"Well, ask for one of our security men to go with you. He will show you where to go and keep you safe."

I didn't like the sound of this. For a start, I didn't want an impromptu guide with me; I liked to wander around by myself, but more worrying was the fact that I possibly needed a security official in the first place. I took a slurp from my bottle. "So, it's that dangerous?"

The barman considered his answer and looked at his watch. "At this time of day, it should be fine. But don't take any valuables with you. Leave your wallet in the hotel safe. And if you take a photo, do it quickly and keep walking. Oh, and don't look anyone in the eyes."

I thanked him, wondering what sort of warzone awaited me beyond the high and impenetrable hotel perimeter fence.

4

Unbeknown to me, the area of Johannesburg I was staying in was Hillbrow. When I had booked the hotel, I simply chose somewhere in the centre of the city, but Johannesburg had many centres, I later discovered, and Hillbrow was only one of them.

Hillbrow was renowned for its unemployment, poverty, drugs and crime. Some people called it a 'gangster paradise'; others called it the 'danger zone'. Most agreed it was as close to 'Dodge City' as any place could be, and easily the most dangerous district in one of the most dangerous cities in the world. In some parts of Hillbrow, gangs had chased residents away from apartment blocks, cleared security guards and installed themselves as illegal slumlords, charging their own rent to immigrants arriving into Johannesburg every day. These 'landlords' kept a tight rein on things, where one missed payment meant a bullet in the head. And according to some reports, the police largely turned a blind eye to the murders, robberies, prostitution rings and rampant drug dealing, preferring instead to accept bribes from crime masters. But not all police officers complied with the drug lords' requests. In 2012, a Hillbrow gang murdered three policemen with knives; they then took the deceased's weapons to shoot and kill four taxi drivers. When police apprehended them, none of the gang showed the slightest remorse. Hillbrow was, as someone succinctly put it, like visiting Somalia, The Congo or Nigeria, without having to leave Johannesburg.

Take the following statistics: in two short years, between 2005 and 2006, Hillbrow saw 246 murders. To put this into context, in the same period, Greater London saw 330 murders, and yet its area is 1445 times bigger than Hillbrow's. So, by using this ratio, if Hillbrow were the same size as London, over 350,000 people would be murdered every year, which is almost a thousand killings a day. So, thank God Hillbrow is contained within a single square kilometre.

Prior to the 1994 elections, Hillbrow had been an affluent, mainly white district, full of upmarket restaurants, fancy apartments and chic hotels. Intellectuals and artists gathered in its cafes, while rich housewives shopped in the malls or had afternoon tea in one of the hotels. In the years after the election, with white flight in speedy motion, the scene was set for the slum it is today. The question was: should I go out and see it?

5

The answer was yes.

As recommended by the barman, I left all my belongings in my room, taking only my camera and a small amount of cash. Before stepping out, I stopped at the hotel desk to ask about safety. The man behind the counter shrugged. "It is okay for now. But don't walk too far from the hotel and, if anyone tries to speak to you, ignore them."

"Do I need a security guard with me?"

The man looked me up and down. "Would you like one?"

"Only if I need one."

The man glanced through the glass doors, though what he could see was scant: outside was just the hotel car park and then a massive security fence. "Just don't walk too far. And be back before dark. You really don't want to be out there at night."

I almost laughed, except it wasn't funny. It sounded like I was in some low-budget horror flick. I thanked the man behind the counter, breathed in, squared my shoulders and stepped outside.

6

Hillbrow wasn't anywhere near as bad as my imagination had made it out to be. But it wasn't much fun, either. Outside the protective gates of the hotel, I decided my sightseeing would be at high speed. To linger over a map or, worse, to pause to take a photo, would only invite attention. I marched past a YMCA building, which looked almost derelict and then almost walked into an overflowing litterbin. Garbage was blowing everywhere, helped by both wind and neglect.

I sidestepped a group of people waiting by the road for a minibus. Most of them were women armed with shopping bags, but some were wiry, thin-eyed men. None looked at me as I passed. As the only white face, though, I felt self-conscious, especially with the hotel's warnings reverberating around my head. Every face was a potential assailant, every shadow harbouring a mugger. It was ridiculous. In Djibouti City and Antananarivo, I had been the only white face. But in those places, I had felt safe.

Not far from the hotel was a tall cylindrical tower called Ponte City. A huge red Vodacom sign was wrapped around the top. Before apartheid, the skyscraper had been one of the most sought-after places to live for affluent whites, marketed as 'Heaven on Earth'. Not now. When the whites moved away, the drug dealers moved in. Ponte City became a hotbed of crime and decay, famous as the Southern Hemisphere's tallest slum, where rubbish was piled so high that it reached the fifth floor.

The 54-storey building before me looked grim and foreboding. Even though the police had flushed most of the drug dealers out and new owners were refurbishing it, Ponte City was an eyesore, a place that epitomised urban decay at its worst. I carried on walking, finding that there wasn't much to see in Hillbrow, apart from neglect. Shops covered with metal bars; endless graffiti and the ever-present piles of litter: the district needed gutting. But then I turned a corner where street-side food stalls specialising in grilled sausages were busy with people. Further on, a woman with a massive shock of Afro-hair was sitting on a pavement stool having her hair fluffed and trimmed by a man with huge hands. Some green-uniformed schoolchildren were laughing on a street corner. Perhaps not all was lost in Hillbrow. But then I came across a large six-storey building where every window was smashed or covered in flyers. One read: manhood enlargements (to reclaim lost lovers).

I walked with false purpose along a busy street, pausing only to gaze at a yellow and grey train thundering across some tracks below me. It was leaving Hillbrow, which was what I wanted to do. A man wearing a thick coat approached. His eyes were hollow and unfocussed. At first I thought he was going to say something, but I realised he wasn't even aware of my presence. I left him to his demons, and then came across a small area of greenery, dominated by the quite ugly Joberg theatre. That was it, I decided: enough was enough. I escaped the mean streets of Johannesburg through the gates of the hotel and retired to my room. I had been outside for less than one hour.

Hillbrow reminded me of a computer game I'd sometimes played as a student. In *SimCity*, if I neglected to give certain areas of my burgeoning city the resources they needed (entertainment districts, employment prospects and a whole host of other things), then that region would fall into decline. If I still ignored the problem, rent dropped, less salubrious businesses moved in and crime rose: exactly what was happening in Hillbrow. The only way to reverse the decline in the computer game was to inject money into the affected region, get rid of poor businesses and add police. I doubted Hillbrow's problems could be solved so easily.

Back in my room, I realised something, though, and Hillbrow had proved this. From my many travels, I had concluded that 99% of people do not even notice or care about a foreigner in their city. They may see them, but they will not hinder them in any way. Of the 1% remaining, the vast majority only want something. Beggars, street hawkers and guides come into this category. Which leaves only a tiny amount of people who wish to do tourists harm. And in over one hundred countries, I had not met one of them.

Later, this thought buoyed me when I thought of my next destination. Against the wishes of my wife and the British foreign office, I was flying to the capital of Tunisia, a city under lockdown. It would be my final stop in Africa before I moved onto Asia. I closed the curtains on Hillbrow and slept soundly.

Clockwise from top left: A panorama of Johannesburg from my hotel balcony; South African rand; The Hillbrow district of Johannesburg is well past its best; The 54-storey Ponte Tower apartment block, once the Southern Hemisphere's tallest slum; Downtown Hillbrow

Chapter 9: Tunis: a city under lockdown!

I touched down at Tunis-Carthage International Airport at a few minutes after 10am. I was the only Westerner passenger on board the Egypt Air jet and I was dog tired. I'd endured an eight-and-a-half-hour flight from Johannesburg to Cairo, then a further two hour hop to the Tunisian capital. I looked outside at the palm trees and terminal building. Tunisia didn't look like a country under lockdown.

But it was.

On 25 June 2015, Seifiddine Rezgui Yacoubi, a 23-year-old radicalised student, entered a beach hotel in the coastal resort of Sousse and began shooting people. As holidaymakers scattered for safety, he calmly, and even jovially, shot them. By the time police killed him, Yacoubi had murdered 38 tourists, most of them British nationals. Three months prior to this heinous event, a group of Islamic State militants attacked the Bardo Museum in Tunis, killing twenty-one, mostly European, tourists. The effect of both these attacks was immediate: tourists stopped going to Tunisia.

Almost a year on, the British Foreign Office still advises its citizens against all but essential travel to Tunisia. They say it is a country in a state of emergency, adding that they do not believe the Tunisian government can 'provide adequate protection for British tourists'. Most Western governments have similar warnings in place.

One of the measures that the Tunisian government did have in place was a curfew. Between the hours of 9pm and 5am, no one could walk the streets of the capital apart from the police and military. This meant I had eleven hours to reach my hotel. I breathed deeply, wondering why I had come to Tunisia.

2

I expected some questions at immigration, but the man in the booth just scanned my passport, stamped it and called the next person.

Twenty minutes later I was in a taxi, staring outside. From what I could gather, the streets of Tunis looked perfectly ordinary. People were going about their business as they did everywhere else in the world. Some walked between palm trees, trying to keep in the shade, others waited in groups for buses. Shops sold goods, children played football and trucks lumbered as they did in every city. There were a few soldiers standing about, all of them with weapons, and there were a few parked police cars between them. For all I knew, that might have been normal for Tunis.

My hotel was on a long stretch of road called Avenue Mohammed V, named after a former king of Morocco. Five months previously, a bus carrying some presidential guards had been travelling along the same road. Close to where my taxi had now stopped, a secret jihadist gained entry to the bus and blew himself up, taking a dozen innocent men with him. Looking outside it was hard to believe such carnage had ever happened.

I paid the driver a few dinar and climbed into the heat. The hotel had security cameras, I noted, and tight-lipped security guards standing near a metal detector. All of them scrutinised me as I entered the lobby.

"Welcome to Tunis," said the young man behind the expansive desk, five minutes later. He handed me my keycard. "We hope you enjoy your stay."

I smiled and took the keycard. So did I, so did I.

Because I was so tired, I dropped my luggage on the floor and flopped down on the bed. When I woke up a few hours later, it was four-thirty, four and a half hours away from the curfew, so I decided to see outside before the sun dropped below the horizon. Behind the hotel was a crisscross of streets with names such as Rue du Yemen, Rue de Monaco, Rue d'Iran and Rue de Pakistan, most of them dusty backstreets featuring small cafes and convenience stores. A teenage boy was selling a handful of pink flowers. Above him, washing dangled from a white apartment block. I passed underneath it, following some people heading towards a small Carrefour minimarket. When no one paid me any attention or tried to kidnap me, I went in and bought myself a bottle of water and a banana. Job done, I returned to the hotel to wait out the lockdown.

3

The hotel restaurant served steak and chips. I sat down to eat my meal while a Tunisian adaptation of *Deal or No Deal* called *Dlilek Mlek* played out on the TV. The format was identical to the UK version, but instead of Noel Edmonds, the presenter was a young Tunisian man in a crimson shirt.

The steak was delicious but I was eating it far too quickly. It reminded me of a recent incident when my wife had cooked some steak, cut it into strips and left it for a few moments. While she busied herself with some sauce, I grabbed a chunk and stuffed it into my mouth. After chewing for a second or two, I swallowed the lump, or tried. It lodged in my throat and the panic was immediate. Unable to speak or breathe, I ran to the fridge and cracked open a can of Diet Coke, hoping to wash the chunk of meat down. Taking a swig, the drink merely frothed about, unable to go anywhere and I started choking, making mute gasping noises. My wife looked at me, unable to comprehend what was happening, and simply stared at the mess of Coke I'd made on the floor. I pointed to my throat as my heart hammered in my chest. I really thought I was going to die. And then I coughed an almighty cough, capable of waking slumbering demons. Nothing happened. I felt my eyes swim and my legs weaken. Finally, my wife realised I was choking to death. I knelt down, waiting for her to do the Heimlich Manoeuvre, but she either didn't know how or wanted me to perish for stealing some steak. In the end, I pushed hard on my abdomen and coughed as hard as I could, this time with superhuman strength. Finally, the piece of hateful meat erupted from my throat and landed on the kitchen floor. We both stared at it for a long while. And, yet, even after all that, I still ate steak too quickly.

Back in my room, I was looking down at Avenue Mohamed V from the safety of my hotel window. It was half past eight and the once-busy thoroughfare was clearing of traffic and people. By the stroke of the hour, the street was deserted. Only flickering streetlights offered any movement. The last time I'd seen such a sudden and dramatic change in the population of a city street had been in Ashgabat, capital of Turkmenistan. But that was a police state. I closed the curtains and began to plan my sightseeing for the next day.

4

The morning was bright and sunny, and Avenue Mohamed V was back to normal. After breakfast, I grabbed my cap and hit the streets of Tunis for what would be my only day in the country. Instead of investigating the backstreets, I strode along the main highway, passing red Tunisian flags, fancy high-rise buildings and people who didn't give me so much as a sideways glance. Except for one person: a young policeman standing at an intersection. He watched me closely but didn't say anything as I passed.

At the end of Avenue Mohamed V was a large roundabout, which formed one end of Place du 14 Janvier 2011, named for the revolution which started that day, a rebellion that overthrew the old regime and kick started the Arab Spring. In the middle of the roundabout stood a tall clock tower that reminded me of slender Big Ben. Tuning right along Avenue Habib Bourguiba, I passed a tiny rectangular park along the way. In the centre was a statue of Ibn Khaldoun, a Tunis-born fourteenth century philosopher. He looked clever, especially with his stern expression, bushy moustache and thick book in his hands. He faced the French Embassy, a grand, pink-orange building that looked like a good place to conduct official business.

Nearby was a large and quite striking cathedral. Built by the French during their colonial days, it was huge, featuring two massively tall columns and an equally large archway. It looked unused and neglected. A large metal gate blocked any access. I found a shaded spot to its left to take stock.

Tunis seemed perfectly safe, or as safe as anywhere in the world could be. I looked at the people going about their business: a headscarfed young woman pushing a pram, an old man with a long grey beard dozing on a wooden chair, two men in business suits sitting in a street-side café, a shop worker loitering outside his jewellery store trying to attract customers – it was all as it ought to be. In times gone by, the long street I was on had been the entertainment district for highbrow French nationals. They built their grand homes, their theatres and their upmarket restaurants along the sweeping lines of the pavement, no doubt trying to replicate the Champs-Élysées, albeit with palm trees. Just along from where I stood was Tunis' famous medina: my next destination.

5

The imposing Bab Bhar marks the start of the medina. The squat stone archway is home to street hawkers, marauding taxi drivers (trying to secure a fare from people leaving the market) and touts. One man sidled up to me while I took a photo. His modus operandi was the tried and tested method of saying hello, asking where I was from and then explaining a little about the monument in front of me. People like him operated all over the world, pouncing on unsuspecting visitors, offering them information before asking for a little something in return. Before the thin man with a blackened tooth had time to fire off his spiel, I shook my head. "Non merci, monsieur," I said with conviction.

The man tutted and walked away, slinking back to whichever shadow he'd emerged from. But then I felt a little sorry for him; after all, tourists were thin on the ground in Tunis. In fact, I was surprised that touts were even operating. Perhaps he'd been a chancer or, more likely, the brother of a carpet seller. Either way, he was gone now and so I entered the labyrinth of lanes and alleys ahead of me.

Leather stalls, carpenters, glassware emporiums, handbag sellers and silk peddlers lined the maze beyond the archway. I was wandering along the Rue de la Kasbah, a name that conjured images of the very sights I was seeing. It reminded me of the souq in Marrakech, except without the tourist hordes. A waft of perfume here, a hint of spice there: the medina was awash with noise and activity.

A teenage boy carting a barrow filled with vats of cooking oil trundled through. I moved over to allow him passage and then continued with my meandering walk, unhindered by any shop front touts. As a single man, they knew I was not interested in silks, perfumes or women's clothes. That said, whenever I allowed my eyes to linger on an arrangement for a second too long, an invite soon followed. *Best price, sir! Best price! Finest silverware for you, my friend.*

I ambled aimlessly, the best thing to do in a rabbit warren. Away from the main strip of stalls, the crowd thinned, with only blacksmiths and painters toiling away inside tiny darkened alcoves. I stopped by a beautiful door, painted bright blue and patterned with black nails and ornate knockers. It was perhaps the most beautiful doorway I'd ever seen, and even the cracked pavement and discarded cigarette ends at its base could not diminish its beauty. Where the portal led, I had no idea. From somewhere came the muezzin's call to prayer. Without the dangling electrical cables, I could have been wandering through medieval Tunisia.

I emerged from a tight lane and stepped into an open area of high walls. The walls belonged to the Al-Zaytuna Mosque, Tunis's oldest. Due to the alleys that surrounded it, the almost two-thousand-year-old place of worship was difficult to see. A tall wall, with some steps cutting through it, led to a balcony. Above the steps, a stout rectangular minaret topped with a golden crescent was just about visible. I decided to investigate.

At the top of the steps was an entrance with a sign saying, 'prayers in progress'. I tried to peer in, but only shadows and reflections met my gaze. Instead, I walked over to the balcony. The view below wasn't that good – just the tops of some tall buildings and a covered entranceway to an alley, but it did have a man bellowing and flapping his arms. Ignoring him, I raised my camera to take a photo, which made him yell in Arabic. Used to this type of behaviour from my visit to Djibouti City, I ignored him, playing the ignorant tourist well. As I took another photo, the man switched to French and then English. "No photo!" he screeched. "Forbidden!"

I lowered my camera and nodded. Then thought, what the hell, and took another photo just to annoy him. It wasn't as if I was taking a photo of people at prayer, or even of the mosque itself: my snaps were of the market below. But then I thought about where I was: Tunis, a city under siege. I was supposed to be keeping a low profile, not annoying the locals. I put my camera away and headed back for the steps. The angry man was already climbing them, red in the face, a wild look in his eyes. I mumbled an apology which unleashed a fresh tirade. Before he had a chance to do anything further, I stepped past him and darted into a busy alleyway.

6

Once past an array of large metal urns and silver kettles, I finally saw some tourists. They were a family of four blonde people with Slavic features. Unlike me, they were dressed to stand out from the crowd. The two teenage girls were wearing tiny shorts and sleeveless T-shirts, a big no-no in the Islamic world. Mum was wearing shorts, too, though longer. Dad was carrying an expensive camera and all of them were gawping at the shops. The proprietors were gawping too, mainly at the women, and I wondered which country they were from, and whether they were aware of the warnings about Tunisia. If they knew about them, they didn't seem to care. I shook my head at their choice of clothing. One of the claims made by ISIS for attacking the holidaymakers in Sousse was that Westerners were degrading and insulting Islam with their decadent ways and sinful clothing. If they saw these four, they would have a field day.

I was getting hot and so decided to find somewhere to get a drink. I chose the El Hana International Hotel simply because it was on my route back to my hotel. It was massive, towering above Avenue de Paris, and when I walked inside its spacious lobby, I headed straight for the elevator. Before getting something to drink, I wanted to visit the top floor to take a photo.

At the top, the doors pinged open and a line of rooms greeted me. In the hope that a window might be around the corner, I traipsed past them but found only more doors. Mentally tutting, I turned tail just as a maid came out of one room. She looked as surprised to see me as I was to see her. Then she smiled and said bonjour.

"Bonjour," I smiled in return, noticing the room she had emerged from had a large window. Perhaps if I were nice, she would allow me to take a quick photo. I smiled again and showed the middle-aged woman my camera, then pointed at the window behind her. She looked, worked out what I wanted and nodded. I then noticed she'd just mopped the floor and so decided not to bother. After all, I didn't want my dusty footprints to ruin her hard work, but she was having none of it, ushering me towards the back of the room, even opening the balcony windows so I could have an unhindered view outside.

The view was glorious, offering a panorama of downtown Tunis, all the way along Avenue Habib Bourguiba to the Mediterranean on my far left. From my eagle's nest, I could see how tree-lined the avenue was, and how relatively flat Tunis was. Opposite me was the theatre, and further over a blue skyscraper. I fired off a series of quick photos, left the balcony, sidestepped the glistening floor as best I could and then thanked the maid for her help and generosity. When I offered her a ten-dinar note (about $5), she waved it away. I insisted, but she shook her head. I dropped the banknote on her trolley and headed for the elevator.

Back down at the lobby level, I found a dingy and smoke-filled bar hidden in a secluded corner of the hotel. Despite the lack of ambient lighting, the bar was busy, full of men with cigarettes and alcohol. I found an empty stool at the bar and ordered a bottle of local beer, Celtia, which had a font that made it look German. I took a thirsty gulp and then looked around at my fellow patrons. All of them looked like locals – perhaps on a lunch break or having business meetings. A few others, like me, were sitting alone, including a thickset man nursing a glass of whisky on the barstool along from me. He noticed me looking and scowled. I turned back to the bar and caught up on emails from the Wi-Fi. When I turned to look, he was still watching me. "You American?" Mr Whisky asked.

"No, British." The man was about thirty, wearing a chequered-blue T-shirt and baggy pants. His waist was spilling over his belt. He didn't look like an Islamic fundamentalist but, then again, who did?

"British? Like Wayne Rooney?"

I smiled. "Yes, just like him."

The man didn't smile back. "Why you in Tunis?"

I decided to keep my answer deliberately vague. "Business."

The man nodded. "Same as me. Dealing with Tunisians is as difficult as doing business with Egyptians. Too much corruption, too much stealing. But there is not much I can do from my office in Cairo. That's why I'm here."

I nodded and downed a healthy gulp of my beer. My new friend took a sip of his drink too, then looked at the barman for a refill. I took this as my cue to leave. I downed my drink and headed back into the blazing sunshine outside.

8

After lunch in the hotel (where another round of *Dlilek Mlek* was running on the TV), I made my way back to the medina, wanting to explore it further. At the start of Rue de la Kasbah, a rib-thin cat scuttled in front of me, a chicken bone in its mouth. It darted into a gap in the stonework, leaving me with the hubbub of bartering and tinny radio music.

I stopped at a stall selling sunglasses. Since breaking them in Djibouti, I'd done without, but with the sun outside, combined with the chance encounter of a stall selling them, I decided to buy some. None of the glasses had prices.

The shop owner, a young man in his early twenties, was upon me in a second. "Very good price, sir. Premium quality merchandise. Please come inside to see the best ones. Special deal for you!"

I seriously doubted that. I pointed at a pair of fake Adidas shades. "How much?"

"Ah for these, the price is..." The man sized me up. "...One hundred dinar. Special price."

I laughed. One hundred dinar was about $50. "I'll give you five dinar."

It was the young man's turn to laugh. "Five dinar! Please give fair price. Five dinar is not fair price and you know it, sir."

I picked up the sunglasses. Someone had stuck a tiny Adidas logo on both arms. The glasses looked cheap, just the type I liked since I kept breaking them. "Ten Dinar, final price," I said.

The man smiled and shook his head, performing his part in the dance. My next step shocked him, though. Instead of the foxtrot, I did a jig and made a move to walk away. The man recovered quickly and lowered his price dramatically. "Thirty dinar."

I turned around. "Ten. That is my final price." I meant it too.

The man asked for twenty, then fifteen, but we finally settled on twelve, about six dollars. I handed over the cash and walked away happy.

I left the covered souq and found myself walking past a beautiful white building decorated in arches and columns. The arches were painted black and white, and behind them, mostly hidden, was a government building. That explained the troops hanging around. Beyond the great building was something even better.

It looked like a ceremonial square. In the middle of it was a white monument surrounded by Tunisian flags. Separate segments made up the piece, all curving upwards towards the centre. I presumed it to be the Independence Monument, which I knew was around here somewhere. As I walked towards it, I noticed the large white building at the far end of the square: it looked governmental. Just as I was wondering whether tourists were allowed in the square, I heard a loud shout to my left. A policeman was coming my way, at speed.

His eyes appraised me. Then he sprouted a whole mouthful of French, none of which I understood. Finally, he switched to English. "Why you here? Go to hotel. Not safe! Not safe for tourist."

I wondered whether there was going to be some sort of demonstration, or if I was simply too visible out in this open square. Whatever the reason, I raised my hands in acquiescence and headed back towards the medina, mingling with the late afternoon crowds. An hour later, I returned to the hotel after a nice day in Tunis.

9

Later that night, as I packed my bag for the umpteenth time, I realised that my time in Africa was almost over. But what an action-packed time I'd had over the last few weeks: Lake Assal in Djibouti, beautiful beaches of Mauritius, the lemurs of Madagascar, the wildlife of Namibia, surviving the slums of South Africa and now experiencing Tunis in this time of great threat. Later, as I watched the streets clear in preparation for the lockdown, I realised how lucky I was to traverse Africa in such a timely and efficient manner. I had dipped my feet into the Dark Continent, and they had come out warm and clean.

But the next portion of my trip promised more adventure and thrills. In South Korea, my plans were to visit the Demilitarized Zone near the North Korean Border. Then I was flying up to the

Mongol plains to stay in Ulaanbaatar. Beijing was next, where I would finally get to walk upon the Great Wall. My journey would end in the tropical paradise of the Maldives: a fitting way to end such a long trip. But first, I had an appointment with a man in Iran.

Clockwise from top left: A beautiful door, one of many, in the medina; A great monument in central Tunis; Minaret of the Al-Zaytuna Mosque; The backstreets near my hotel; Wandering towards the clock tower; Inside the medina; Glitz and red flag of downtown Tunis; An old man contemplates life during the lockdown

Part 2

Asia

Iran, South Korea, Mongolia, China, Maldives

Chapter 10: Kish Island: the easy part of Iran

To be honest, I was a little nervous about visiting the Islamic Republic of Iran. Aside from the possibility of police detainment, there was also the threat of kidnap. In 2007, Robert Levinson, an American private investigator, disappeared while visiting Kish Island and hasn't been seen since. Nothing, not a whisker. Even so, I was intrigued by the Middle Eastern nation. Every report I'd read about it, aside from the ones about kidnappings, nuclear weapons and Ayatollahs, was positive, especially about the friendly folk who lived there. I just had to see it for myself.

With only one day set aside for visiting Iran before jetting off to South Korea, I knew going to the mainland was out of the question: the visa hurdles were just too cumbersome. No, the only way was to fly to a place called Kish Island (pronounced Keesh), an Iranian free zone, where a visitor could procure a 14-day visa on arrival, free of charge, without any burdensome formalities whatsoever. Glitzy hotels, shopping malls and lush beaches would greet me when I got there. The Iranians' wish was to make Kish Island their Dubai.

The only way to reach Kish Island from outside Iran is to fly from Dubai. Kish Air runs a series of scheduled flights every day and, if I booked sensibly, I could be on the island by 11am, see the sights and be out by 8.45pm: plenty of time to see an island three times smaller than the city of York.

Kish Air flights are popular with workers from the United Arab Emirates, mainly Filipino visa runners living in Dubai. Every month or so, they leave the UAE because their visas are about to expire. To get a new one, Dubai immigration has to stamp them out of the country, which then allows them to fly to the cheapest different country. After 24 hours, they can fly back into Dubai to collect another visa. A nice little industry has grown up around these visa runners, with quick thinking Iranian companies on Kish organising airport transfers and cheap hotels for these short term visitors.

Located in the bowels of Dubai Airport's Terminal 2 is a tiny office belonging to Kish Airlines. For anyone living outside of Iran, visiting the office is the only way to buy flight tickets. The Filipino woman behind the desk seemed efficient, tapping away on her computer. She told me there was a seat for me on the next day's flight. "But why you go to Kish for only one day?" she asked.

I had my excuse ready; I would probably be asked the same thing when I arrived on Kish Island. "My wife is shopping in Dubai and I can't face that – so I've decided to visit Kish instead."

"So holiday is purpose of visit?"

I nodded and she wrote something down on a form. After I handed over 699 Emirati dirham (about £100), she gave me a printed-out piece of paper showing that I was booked on a return Kish Airlines flight the next morning. I thanked the woman and caught a taxi into downtown Dubai for the night.

2

The next morning, I was at the airport good and early. As predicted, the vast majority of my fellow passengers were Filipinos. The women chatted animatedly while the men flicked through websites on their phones. All the women had free-flowing locks, which they would have to cover with headscarves upon arrival in Iran. As well as the Filipinos, there was a troop of young Sri Lankan men in dark suits. Most of the suits were ill fitting – too big and wide. The men seemed too young to be businessmen and I was intrigued about why they were going to Kish. The answer came a few minutes later when one of them stood up and I caught sight of a badge on his lapel. They belonged to a Dubai-based snooker club flying to a billiards competition on the island.

The Kish Airlines jet arrived: a colourful but older jet that had seen better days. When the call to board came, we all did, trudging along a cabin engraved with Alitalia markings. When I located my assigned seat, a headscarved woman in a Kish Air uniform yelled at me to move to the rear. When I protested, pointing out my seat number, she yelled even more. "Move to back. Any seat. Go!" While I scarpered, she yelled at another man. When he looked blankly at her, she flipped her lid and shoved him towards the rear. He ran for his life. Then she yelled at a Filipino woman who was trying to sit down near the front. She was the angriest stewardess in the world, and her colleague further along was almost as bad.

Even so, the flight was full and, once we were airborne, a sandwich was thrust my way, and then, before I had time to settle down or consider how stupid it was to be flying into Iran, we landed. It had taken thirty minutes to fly across the Arabian Gulf to our destination.

Exiting the aircraft was a novel experience. Instead of departing from the side door as normal, a hatch at back opened, and a ramp lowered to the tarmac. A set of small steps let us directly beneath the tail.

Kish Airport was small. The queue for immigration was long, though, giving me the chance to study my surroundings. We were in a rectangular room heading towards the one and only security official in the building. Most of the Filipino women had already donned headscarves, which they must have brought themselves. They were all chatting away, laughing and joking; no one seemed apprehensive, apart from me. The immigration officer was working quickly and, when it was my turn, I steeled myself for some hard questioning: after all, I was the only Westerner in sight. The man looked at me, took my passport and then started turning through each page. Any sign of an Israeli stamp, and he would refuse me entry. While he searched, I regarded the young girl in the booth with him. She was aged about six and had a colouring book and some crayons. She looked like his daughter. The man's eyes flicked upwards. A second later, he stamped my passport and handed it back. That was it: I was free to enter Iran. *Welcome to Beautiful Kish Island*, a large sign read.

"So glad you made it," beamed Rahim, my guide for the day. His accent was thick but understandable. "I told you immigration would be easy for you."

Rahim was about thirty years old, clean-shaven with a Western-type haircut and clothes. He looked nothing like the Ayatollah or any of his robed and bearded cronies. He had been living in Kish for five years now, after escaping the big city of Tehran.

I shook his hand, smiling. I'd secured Rahim's service after an internet search a few days previously. Tour guides on Kish Island were thin on the ground, I'd quickly discovered, and Rahim was the only one who had returned any of my emails. After reassuring me that Kish Island was safe, and that Islamic extremists would not kidnap me, he described the many things I would see. After that, we had arranged to meet up.

Just then, his phone rang. As we walked towards his car, Rahim began chatting away to someone in thick Farsi. A minute later, he finished his call and apologised. "Just a colleague from work. They want to know why the computer systems are down. I told them yesterday, but they do not listen. And I am the boss!"

"Oh, so you're the boss of the tour company?"

"Tour company? No, I work in an IT department. I only show tourists around in my spare time. Today, I told my colleagues that my car needed a service and so I would be out all day – but still they ring me! This is the tenth call this morning. I hope you don't mind me taking them."

The airport road was pristine, light in traffic but busy with billowing green, white and red Iranian flags. Large shrubs, punctuated with tiny red flowers, lined the road. I might have been in Dubai or perhaps Kuala Lumpur: everything looked deliciously tropical and clean. Further on, perched above a roundabout packed with palm trees, was a large billboard depicting the Ayatollah

Khomeini. It reminded me instantly that I was in the Islamic Republic of Iran.

"Tell me," said Rahim, "what religion are you?"

I bristled at the question. I didn't know how to answer. It seemed rude even to ask. Was it bad to admit being a lapsed Christian? Was it worse to lie and say I was a Muslim? Outside, the streets of Kish were quiet. A huge, blue-glassed building was on our right, emblazoned with 'Kish Trade Centre' on its front. It looked like a shopping mall. In the end, I decided to answer truthfully. "I was born a Christian, but stopped going to church when I was ten. So I have no religious beliefs."

Rahim nodded thoughtfully. "Same as me. I was born Muslim – and still am – but I do not follow teachings of Islam like my parents do in Tehran. For a start, I like beer."

This revelation really surprised me – not just that Rahim drunk alcohol, but that the regime even allowed it on Kish. "I thought Iran was a dry country?" I said.

"It is, but if you want beer, I can get some for you. But there is a catch. It costs $20 for one can of Heineken. People smuggle it in from Dubai by boat. But there is lots of non-alcoholic beer in Iran. Every shop in Kish sells it. I will buy some for you later. It is my favourite drink – except for real beer, of course."

4

Our first stop on the Kish Island sightseeing extravaganza was a place called Kariz, an ancient underground city that the Lonely Planet described as a 'commercially-driven complex masquerading as a historical site.' Rahim thought differently, telling me that, although the site *had* been modernised to attract visitors, the central section – a pre-Islam hydraulic well system known as a qanat – was over a thousand years old and well worth a visit.

"Kish Island is made of coral," he told me as we pulled into the empty car park. "The people who lived here thousands of years ago dug into the coral and made wells and tunnels. When it rained, fresh water filtered down through the well, and by the time it got to bottom part of qanat, it was pure enough to drink. This is how people survived in such an arid place. Come, I will show you."

We both climbed down some circular stone steps into the catacombs. Once underground, Kariz did look a little showy and false. It was atmospherically lit and it had a man's voice speaking in a Farsi monotone filtering in through hidden speakers, presumably explaining what I was seeing. It also had a cafe and a gift shop, but it did have the central qanat, a chimney-like vent, which, as Rahim had explained, cut vertically through the coral to strike the surface and open air above our heads.

"In ancient times," Rahim told me as we wandered past a deep chasm resonant with the sound of running water, "the channels were so large that sheeps could use it."

I was astonished. Why would a sheep use a water channel? "Sheep? Down here?"

Rahim nodded solemnly. "Of course. Many sheep."

It was only later I realised he meant ship.

Another section of the underground city was full of pottery and pieces of woven cloth. Rahim tried his best to explain the importance of them, but to me, a pot was a pot, and it didn't matter whether it was from the Neolithic period or from IKEA – it held no interest. I was a heathen of the highest order. Perhaps sensing my impatience, Rahim said we would head back up to ground level.

5

Back on the road, I asked Rahim where he had learnt to speak English. We were driving along a palm-fringed highway that featured plenty of cranes and construction. Kish Island, it seemed, was going through a building boom.

"School," he said. "Everyone has to learn it in Iran." We were now passing another large billboard of the Ayatollah. With his large white beard and fierce expression, he looked a man not to be trifled with. Rahim glanced at me. "Why? Is my English not good for you?"

I told him I was impressed by it.

"Thank you. So let me ask you something. When you are sitting in nice chair, how would it feel?"

It was an unusual question, and I had no clue how to answer it. Rahim could see I was confused, so he tried again. "Okay, if you were sitting in nice chair, would you be aching or would you feel . . ." He left the sentence hanging, waiting for me to finish it.

"...comfortable?"

"Yes! Comfortable! That is the correct way of saying it. But when I was at school, our teacher told us it was pronounced 'comfort – table', you know, like table in a house. So that is how I said it for many years until I met someone from England. And he said it like you just did. So what I'm saying is this: I think I speak English well, but sometimes I will say something wrong – but I am blaming my old English teacher, a man who never set foot outside Tehran in his life. I can hear him now - Ajus–table, collec–table, regret–table."

Another case in point came up a few minutes later. At the side of the road, travelling at some speed was a man on a horse. I pointed him out to Rahim, who nodded absently. "Yes, people on Kish ride the cow often."

6

Our next stop was an upmarket establishment called the Darioush Grand Hotel, the plushest hotel on the island, Rahim told me. In the winter months, the hotel was full of rich Iranian tourists from the mainland. "Thousands of them pack the resort hotels and shopping malls all over Kish; week after week they come. My parents sometimes come, too. They stay with me and my brother to escape the smog and traffic of Tehran."

The hotel lobby was as opulent as it was expansive. Based on the ancient Persian civilisation of Persepolis, its high walls featured authentic-looking carvings and bas-reliefs while stone statues guarded its entrance. A trio of businessmen were at one end of the lobby, sitting on chairs large enough to be thrones. Rahim and I walked past them, heading towards a door at the far end. Through the other side, at the rear of the hotel, was a large garden of sorts. Winged stone beasts flanked the pathway, together with a huge statue of Darius the Great, for whom the hotel was named. When Darius was alive, he ruled over one of the greatest empires Persia has ever seen, a land that stretched from Egypt in the south, the Balkans in the north and then enveloped the Middle East as far as the Caucasus.

"How much is it to stay here?" I asked Rahim. We had stopped at a series of waterfalls and stone columns. If I ignored the construction work going on in the distance, that even the multitude of palm trees could not hide, I could've been in a Biblical version of paradise.

"For one room, I think $150. Very expensive. But if you ever want to come back to Kish and stay here, let me know. I get good price for you."

7

It was time for lunch, and the establishment Rahim chose was the Paris International Restaurant. It had a plastic mock-up of the Eiffel Tower outside. It was next door to Chi Chiz, a falafel-kebab cafe, which was next door to another small eatery. There were no McDonald's or Pizza Huts in Iran, but Rahim told me there was a KFC on the island: Kish Fried Chicken.

Waiting inside the almost empty restaurant for us was Rahim's younger brother, Mehdi. He was in his mid-twenties, slightly overweight, but in possession of the same friendly features as his elder sibling. He stood up and shook my hand, heartily. "Welcome to Kish, my friend. I hope you are enjoying our hospitality."

Mehdi told me he worked at the same office as his brother. Rahim was a good boss, he added. "But he is sometimes lazy. He makes us do all the work while he reads the newspaper."

The three of us sat down at a diner-type table so we could peruse the menu. Since it was in Farsi, I just looked at the photos. At the front, a couple of waiters hovered expectantly.

One of them came over, a thin man in his early sixties with a greasy apron and permanent grin. He spoke to Rahim while eyeing me. Eventually, all three of us opted for turkey pizzas, which, Rahim assured me, were the best thing on the menu. We also ordered some soft drinks, the only drinks available. When the old man walked away, Rahim told me that he was actually the owner. "He wants to shake your hand later. He doesn't get many Western visitors in his restaurant and wants to thank you for choosing his."

A few minutes later, he returned with our drinks. Both Rahim and Mehdi had ordered cans of non-alcoholic beer. Mine was a diet coke, which came in a wine glass. I stood up and shook the man's proffered hand. He babbled at me in Farsi while I smiled and shrugged. He then produced a camera and took my picture. Then I had to stand next to him while Rahim took another. When the pizzas came, all of us tucked in with gusto. After a few slices, I asked the brothers how long they planned to live on Kish Island for.

Rahim answered first. "I have thought about moving to Australia. We have a cousin who works in Melbourne." Mehdi nodded, grabbing another slice of pizza. "He is a computer programmer and earns big money – more than we could ever earn in Iran. But here's the thing: he tells us he works all hours, even weekends. He hardly sees his wife and son and he never gets to enjoy the beach. So when I hear this, I think that maybe Kish is better for us. We have money to enjoy ourselves and our work does not kill us. That is worth something, I think."

Mehdi nodded. "I am happy here. I do not want to move anywhere."

The owner came over again and spoke to the brothers, glancing at me while he did so. I guessed he was asking whether I thought the pizza was okay. It was, and I gave him a thumbs-up. The man beamed and shook my hand again. He was the friendliest cafe owner I'd met in all my travels.

I noticed a collection of about thirty small flags arranged on the front counter. I scanned them, looking for the Union Jack, but couldn't see it. I pointed this out to Rahim, who looked, and then addressed the old man. The man looked stricken. He then spoke to Rahim for a short while.

Rahim looked at me. "He says British flag is in back, in a drawer with an American one. He used to have both flags there but police told him to remove them. They said the flags belonged to enemy countries. But he will put them back for you, if you wish. He says you are a friend of Iran and if you want to see your flag, then he will get it."

I told him not to go to such lengths. I wasn't bothered about the lack of a British flag; I'd just been wondering why it hadn't been there. Now I knew. The man grinned some more and then returned to the kitchen.

8

Rahim seemed intrigued by how I said the word "Ayatollah". We were sitting in another hotel, the Shayan International, having a coffee. Ten minutes previously, we had dropped Mehdi off at their shared apartment. Instead of going back to work, Mehdi decided to have an afternoon siesta. No wonder they didn't want to move to Australia: they had the life of Riley on Kish. But before saying goodbye, he had insisted we swap telephone numbers because we were, as he put it, brothers.

"Say it again," Rahim asked, smiling.

I picked up the 100,000-rial note again, which was worth about three dollars. On the front was an image of the long-bearded man himself: the Ayatollah Khomeini, the old revolutionary leader who had founded the Islamic Republic of Iran in 1979. I said his name, much to the continued amusement of Rahim.

"Say it again."

"What's so good about me saying it?" I asked, taking a sip of my hellishly hot coffee.

"You sound funny saying it. I don't know why."

"Am I saying it wrong?"

"No. Just not right."

Back on the road, the realisation hit me that I was now completely at ease about being in Iran. Everyone was friendly, just as I had read they would be. The perceived danger was non-existent. Iran was possibly the safest place I'd visited.

We were passing through another main street of the town. Headscarved young women wandered along, keeping to the shade offered by the palm trees. Young men chatted in cafes. We passed a giant sculpture of a black and white penguin, which was next to a massive metal pineapple. Further on, we drove by a massive building shaped like an ocean liner. Rahim told me it was going to be a restaurant.

We pulled over by the side of the road near a bank. I wanted to change some of my Emirati dirhams into Iranian rials so I could have a memento of my visit to Kish. When I stepped into the bank, Rahim seemed to know everyone, shaking hands with almost every man inside. A tall man approached and shook hands with Rahim. He was the manager. I shook hands too, and he ushered me into a back office and invited me to sit down. A minute later, an underling brought a tray of tea. I took a cup and wondered what was going on.

"Iran welcomes you, sir," the manager said. "And I personally hope you are enjoying your time on Kish Island."

I nodded, which brought a fresh round of handshakes.

"Well, since you are a friend of Iran, we will provide you with some rials at a generous exchange rate." I passed over a hundred-dirham note and the manager shouted for another minion and explained what I wanted. The newcomer nodded and set to work. Five minutes later, he returned with a wad of crispy rials. Rahim took one and pointed to the man on the front. It was the Ayatollah.

"Say his name." He shot a glance at the bank manager, as if to say, listen to this.

I said the name again, wondering what it was about my pronunciation that was causing so much amusement. The manager's eyes widened and then he laughed too. "You have heard of this man?"

I nodded. "I thought everyone had heard of him."

He looked at Rahim. "Amazing. Truly Amazing!"

On the way out, I stopped to shake hands with another set of bank workers, ranging from clerks to tea boys. All of them wanted to shake hands with the man from England. Iran was the friendliest country in the world: of that, I had no doubt.

9

On the northern coast of Kish lies the old town of Harireh. Not much remains because, 800 years ago, an earthquake demolished it. I was surprised to find a few Filipino tourists wandering the ruins, but Rahim explained that their visa-run tours usually included a free excursion, and many chose Harireh because it was close to the hotels.

It was most likely free because there wasn't much to see: just piles of rubble, a few reconstructed walls showing the layout of the old houses, a few arches and the odd tower. But what it lacked in history, it more than made up for in its views. We stood on the edge of a perilous cliff and gazed out at an expanse of crystal-clear azure ocean, unbroken except for a few ships and an indistinct outline of brown: the coast of the mainland, just over ten miles away. Kish Island has one of the best coastlines in the Gulf region, and to my right, on the tip of a headland, developers were taking full advantage. A new hotel complex looked like it was nearing completion.

A whirring engine shattered the sound of gentle waves. Both Rahim and I looked up to see a gyrocopter, its flimsy rotor blades and toboggan-like body zipping through the air about a hundred feet above our heads. The passenger waved and so we did the same back. Then it was out over the sea. When I looked to my left, I could see a paraglider floating above a long stretch of sand. Kish Island *was* like Dubai, sort of.

We walked towards a small cafe and came across a couple of young Filipino men walking in the opposite direction. Rahim stopped to chat. He found out that Rodel and Albert were from Manila and worked as waiters in Dubai. They were doing a visa run, their fifth since they had arrived in the Middle East.

"Do you know something?" said one of the men. "In Dubai, the locals never stop to talk to us, do they?" His friend nodded in accord. "They treat us like second-class citizens. But here, it's different. People always stop to talk to us."

The cafe was almost full. I found a table while Rahim bought some refreshments, which turned out to be cans of non-alcoholic beer. While we toasted ourselves, my phone vibrated. It was a *WhatsApp* message from Rahim's brother, Mehdi. He was asking who my favourite rock group were. When I replied with Queen, he answered by saying his favourite artist was ageing crooner, Chris de Burgh. In case I didn't know who he meant, Mehdi had attached a photo. I showed it to Rahim, who nodded. "My brother loves Chris de Burgh. I do, too. He is very popular in Iran. Everyone loves him. His records sell many millions and he is always on TV. One day, I would like to see him perform in the real life."

I could hardly credit it. In the UK, Chris de Burgh was largely forgotten, but in Iran, he was a megastar. While I pondered this, Rahim made a phone call, presumably to his place of work, just as another message arrived from Mehdi. Again, it had an accompanying photo, which I couldn't yet see, but the message was shocking enough. It read: *My beautiful cock!*

I involuntarily covered my phone's screen before Rahim could see it. Where the hell had that come from? From Chris de Burgh to an indecent proposal in just one message. I was so flummoxed, I almost dropped my phone on the floor. When Rahim took a hearty swig from his can, I surreptitiously scrolled down and laughed. Mehdi had sent a photo of a chicken. Another message popped up: *And my gorgeous partridge*. Thank God for that. I showed the partridge and chicken to Rahim.

"My brother loves that chicken. We bought it for food but we can never kill it now."

10

Half an hour later, we were driving westwards towards Kish Island's star attraction: the Greek Ship. As we whizzed along a coastal road, I noticed a gigantic Iranian flag swaying at the top of a massive flagpole. But there was something else, too: a strikingly tall sculpture. I asked Rahim if we could stop and he happily obliged. The sculpture turned out to be one of the most beautiful statues I'd seen in all my travels. It depicted a grey-winged human-type figure holding a lantern, pointing it out to sea. It towered above me like an angel, or a monster – I couldn't work out which. Its gaunt stone face stared out across the sea too, rather like a human form of lighthouse.

"What is it?" I asked, staring up at the wonder. If there was a gift shop selling small representations of the statue, I might have bought one, but there was not. Kish Island was missing a trick, I felt.

Rahim shrugged. "I'm not sure. But it's new. To be honest, I don't know anything about it. But come, my friend. We must get to the Greek ship before I return you to the airport."

On a hot July day in 1966, just four days before England beat Germany in a famous World Cup Final, a few observant residents of Kish Island watched a large cargo ship approach the coastline.

Instead of turning away, as ships usually did, the vessel carried on towards the shore, heading to the shallows and sandbanks. As the people watched, the ship creaked to a watery halt seventy metres from the coast. The ship, the Greek-owned Khoula F, had been on its way to Athens when this easily avoidable disaster happened. And despite the best efforts of tugs and salvage teams, the ship could not be moved. It has remained in place ever since.

A park had grown up around Kish Island's favourite tourist attraction. It featured benches, parasols, randomly-located boulders and a couple of enterprising men offering camel rides. As well as this, there was a large nautically-themed wooden wheel and a few professional photographers. It was deliciously touristy, and I loved it.

Unlike everywhere else in Kish, with the exception perhaps of the shopping malls, the Greek Ship could draw a crowd. Many of the people wandering around or sitting facing the sea were families with children, the women headscarfed and covered, the children in fancy clothes. One young woman manoeuvred herself to a rocky outcrop, tottering on high heels until she found a suitable perch. She pouted while her father took a photo. Behind her was the ship.

Even though its hull was rusted and full of holes, stained in every shade of brown and orange, and despite its ruptured deck, the Greek Ship was a magnificent sight to behold. It was so big, for a start. And it looked like it needed to be in a graveyard, especially with its cross-like metal masts standing sentinel above the rotting and gigantic hulk. It was easily the best thing I'd seen on Kish and I told Rahim this.

"I'm pleased you like it. Most people agree it is best thing on Kish, though, to me, it's just a broken ship that the ocean is slowly taking as its own. In twenty years, the Greek Ship will be gone, and these people will be staring at waves."

"But by then," I said, "Kish will be full of five-star hotels and no one will care."

"I think you are right."

It was time to head back to the airport in the centre of the island. It only took ten minutes. Rahim insisted on waiting with me until I was at passport control. Just before I left, I shook hands with my new Iranian friend. He and his fellow islanders had been nothing but hospitable to me from the moment I arrived. "Next time," he said, "bring your wife, bring your friends; Let the world know about Kish Island and the Iranian people."

I said goodbye, shook Rahim's hand again and passed through security. Forty minutes later, I was taking off into darkness. The bright lights of Dubai were on the horizon. After a night in Dubai, I would be South Korea bound.

My beautiful cock.

And my partridges.

Clockwise from top left: An amazing statue on Kish Island; Rahim and me enjoying some non alcoholic beverages in the Paris International Restaurant; Do you want to see my beautiful cock?; Kish looks like the Maldives; The old town of Harireh; The Ayatollah Khomeini on the 100,000-rial banknote; Leaving by the rear hatch of the Kish Air jet; Kish Island's greatest tourist site – the Greek Ship

Chapter 11: Seoul searching in South Korea

Approaching Seoul's Incheon International Airport was like flying over England. Beneath the extensive layer of cloud, a wide selection of waterlogged green fields, low-lying hills and forest clumps stretched to the horizon. The metropolis of Seoul, the fourteenth largest city in the world (and Asia's most liveable place, according to a survey carried out in 2015), was somewhere on my right, but in the mist and gloom, I couldn't see it. And then we were flying over water – the Yellow Sea, no less. As we turned towards our final approach, Korea looked distinctly grey.

Incheon Airport processed me in twenty minutes: a miraculous amount of time for such a large airport. But because it lies fifty kilometres from the centre of Seoul, getting to the city would take some time. I ignored the wallet-busting taxis, which wanted to charge me 70,000 won (£50) for the one-way journey, and instead opted for the much cheaper limousine bus. Standing at the queue, I shivered with my fellow passengers. Even though it was April, Seoul was shaking off the last remnants of winter. After the tropical heat of Africa, Asia – at least in the Korean peninsula – was bitter. While I considered how cold Mongolia might be, the limousine bus pulled up.

I handed over 15,000 won to an employee of the bus company, the two banknotes that made up the amount bearing impressively moustachioed and wispy-bearded men, and then climbed aboard. Unlike a regular bus, the grandiose limousine bus featured a reclining seat and spacious legroom. I flopped down behind a teenage boy watching an anime cartoon on his large smartphone (he seemed utterly engrossed), and then I started wondering about something. When I reached Seoul city centre, how would I know which stop to alight from? All I had was a route map of the stops and an email the hotel had sent, neither of which seemed sufficient now. I studied the map. The stop I had to watch out for was *Jongno3-ga*. As well as Jongno3-ga, there were many other Jongno stops on the route, all with different numbers. Would it be obvious when I reached the third one? I had no idea. But with nothing else in my box of plans, I had no choice but to hope for the best.

2

Evening was settling in across the southern Korean Peninsula, and the lights were coming on across the city. Thirty minutes into the journey, the skyscrapers of Seoul appeared: a forest of gleaming office buildings and company headquarters, interspersed with dancing neon billboards and cascading sparkles. Seoul reminded me of Tokyo or Hong Kong. The only natural feature I could see was the Han River to my left, a wide expanse of grey traversed by a series of low-level bridges. Rushing across them were cars and buses, mostly Kias or Hyundais.

An hour after leaving the airport, we reached central Seoul. The bus stopped and a few people got off. I looked at the bus stop, but it was all in Korean. At the next stop, where even more passengers alighted, I tried to look for landmarks. I didn't recognise a thing, but then again, why would I? I had never been to Seoul before. As we moved off, moving slowly in the traffic of downtown, all I could see were tall office buildings, rows of shops and towering skyscrapers.

At the next stop, I peered out, hoping to see something that said Jongno; any of the Jongno stops would do now. But there was no indication of the word anywhere. In desperation, I talked to the woman across the aisle. She couldn't understand what I was saying, even when I pointed to the route map. When she turned back to the front, I decided to take drastic action. When the bus slowed for the next stop, I waited in the aisle. I would get off and work out where I was. Just then, the bus shuddered to a stop. I almost fell backwards, but managed to grab onto the safety bar just in time. It reminded me of an embarrassing incident from my childhood, a memory that perhaps explains my aversion to buses.

Aged eleven, I had to catch my weekly bus to the main swimming pool in the centre of Middlesbrough, Northern England. I could have walked, but that would have taken over an hour in the dark, and I could have caught a lift with my dad, but he hardly ever offered. I hated catching that bus, jammed in a seat between people going to work or gossiping like old ladies, which they mostly were. One particular occasion will stay with me forever. My stop was coming up and I was walking up the aisle. With my large bag (crammed to capacity with a towel, swimming gear, packed lunch, homework books and stupidly large pencil case), my equilibrium was already perilous. When the bus suddenly lurched to a dramatic – almost emergency style – stop and then inexplicably reversed. I lost my balance and flew backwards. This would have been exquisitely embarrassing in itself, but what made it worse was my landing spot, for it was in the lap of a buxom, blue-rinse pensioner, my head cushioned protectively between her enormous and cuddly-soft bosom. As everyone looked dumbstruck, my eleven-year-old self was mortified. I righted myself, mumbled an apology to Betty (she looked like a Betty), and scurried towards the front of the bus, embarrassment singeing my every pore. At the exit, I braved a sneak at the pensioner, who didn't look bothered in the slightest, and then escaped into the shadows of Middlesbrough city centre. Back in Seoul, thirty years on, I no longer felt the keen embarrassed of an eleven-year-old boy, and even managed to smile a little as I stepped onto the pavement.

3

I watched the bus leave. Then I looked at the bus stop. Written in tiny letters was the word Jongno. Whether it was Jongno1, Jongno2, Jongno3 or any of the Jongnos up to 6, I had no idea. I dug around in my pockets for the printed instructions the hotel had sent by email. It read: *Please get off bus at Jongno3-ga stop. In the opposite direction as the bus departs, walk approximately 50m.* Without a better plan, I decided to do as they asked.

I looked along the street. How far was fifty metres? I knew one pace was about one metre, or at least thought so, and so set off walking, passing the humanity of downtown Seoul: businessmen with brief-cases and umbrellas, couples walking hand in hand, women with shopping bags and, in dark alcoves, a few homeless people. A high proportion of people were wearing flu masks, I noticed, heeding warnings about pollution from China passing over their city. There were also plenty of cheap jewellery shops and groups of schoolchildren. It appeared that schools in Korea finished later than their English counterparts, because it was close to 5.30pm.

After fifty steps, I stopped and sniffed the air for clues. The instructions said to turn right at the intersection. The problem was, no intersection existed, but there was one further along. Perhaps I'd miscalculated my steps, so I walked another thirty and then turned right, waiting patiently with everyone else for the green man to flash. Countries where pedestrians waited for the green man, rather than springing across whenever the fancy took them were more civilized, I'd discovered. Japanese people waited, German people waited, and so did people from Sweden, and now South Korea. On the other hand, Russians barged across the road, and so did people from England.

Finally, I got across, spying a whole row of chophouses to my left, dangling chickens in their windows plucked clean and sorry-looking. An old man was flogging digital watches from a tiny stand by the side of the road. He was wrapped like an Eskimo, hands deep into his pockets. Passing him, I doggedly followed the instructions (which now said, walk straight for five minutes), even though I knew deep down I had already gone wrong. At one point, I stopped near a homeless man, his wispy beard making him look like an ageing Karate master, to scour the street for something called Nagwon Ttoek-jib. Whether it was a building, a street name or a landmark, I had no idea, but the hotel's instructions said it should be visible. It wasn't.

I dropped a coin in the homeless man's tin and read the penultimate sentence in the instructions: *Take the side street from Nagwon Ttoek-jib, and the hotel is 100m on the left.* I took the first side street I came to and walked past a music shop, then a shop selling, among other things, a hideous gold lamé jacket. I couldn't linger, though; the chill of winter was closing in and I wanted to find the damned hotel. Sighing, I dragged my luggage down a thin alley and then admitted to myself that I was well and truly lost.

4

It should have taken ten minutes to reach the hotel from the bus stop. I looked at my watch. It was thirty-five minutes since I had alighted from the bus. It was dark by now, and all I wanted was to find the bloody hotel. I stopped a man pushing a bicycle. He looked about seventy and listened to my request for help with mute confusion in his eyes. Then he shook his head and walked off. I even asked the old geezer selling watches. I showed him the bus route map, tapping my finger on the Jongno3-ga stop. He looked but shrugged. If I was not interested in buying one of his watches, then he was not interested in helping me.

Thanks a lot, I thought bitterly, heading back to the main road to find a taxi. Once there, I stuck my arm out, but none of the sleek Hyundais whizzing by stopped. Perhaps Seoul was one of those cities where people had to pre-book taxis, or maybe the drivers were all swine. In desperation, I switched on data roaming on my phone, even though it probably cost $100/hour. I typed in the name of the hotel. *It didn't exist!* How could a hotel not exist? I felt like throwing my luggage into the air and yelling at the top of my lungs. I was stranded in a foreign city, and it was entirely my fault for trying to save a few quid by not getting an airport taxi.

I walked along the road until I turned off into a neon-lit alleyway busy with street food stalls. Most of them were selling orange rice cakes, sausage chunks, woks of stir-fry and endless meaty things stuck onto skewers. Street and dangling shop signs were all in Korean. I stopped a man aged about thirty, asking him whether he could speak English. He could, but he didn't know where the hotel was, but he had heard of it, he added helpfully. A slightly older man must have heard our exchange because he stopped. "Hotel over there," he said. "Not far. He was pointing to my left, behind a row of tall shops. "Go down there, then left, then right. You find hotel."

I thanked both men profusely and set off, turning left at the first street I came to, then right at the next. And there it was: the Ibis Seoul Insadong, a tall building near a 7-Eleven store, surrounded by other tall buildings. It had only taken one hour and twenty-five minutes to find.

5

The Ibis was the first hotel I'd stayed in to have two abseiling kits as part of the standard-issue room equipment. There was also a fire extinguisher and an emergency flashlight. I took a moment to study the instructions on the box of the *Simplicity Descending Life Line*. Most of the writing was in Korean, but some was in English. The first instruction said to hang the hook (presumably the hook was inside the box) over the supporting ring. I found the supporting ring sticking out from the wall near the window. Next was to fasten the belt around my waist. Third was to throw the rope out of the window, and finally, heave myself out, descending safely as I faced the wall. I looked down from the window. It was dark, but I could tell I was bloody high off the ground, on the twelfth floor, no less. It would be terrifying abseiling out of the window, but with flames licking around my heels, I would probably be willing to try it.

Grappling hooks, ropes and fire-fighting equipment were common in Korean hotels and highrise buildings thanks to a couple of dreadful hotel fires. The first was on Christmas Day, 1971 at the Taeyunkak Hotel in downtown Seoul, an establishment, like many others of that era, that did not feature much in the way of emergency fire-fighting equipment. As the inferno raged inside the hotel, causing temperatures to reach 700-degrees Celsius, people were trapped in their rooms. One man jumped from an upper-storey window holding onto a mattress. A black and white photo exists of him after he had just jumped. Behind him, noxious smoke is billowing out of every window. He died on the pavement below, joining the other 163 people who lost their lives that day in South Korea's worst fire-related accident. Thirteen years later, there was a second fire, this one in Pusan, South Korea's second biggest city. Even though helicopters managed to pull a few people from the roof, and fire fighters rescued a few more via ladders, 37 people died of smoke inhalation whilst trapped in their upper-storey rooms. Since then, all hotels in South Korea are required to have abseiling equipment.

The toilet in the bathroom was as futuristic as I hoped it would be. This one, called the Blooming NB-1160, featured lots of buttons and dials, including: a pulsating rinse (to promote blood circulation), a special antibacterial oscillating nozzle (front and back), a specially heated seat and then something called, 'hot air drying (high and low power)'. At night, LED lighting would mean there would be no near misses. Feeling in need of some pampering, I sat in the cockpit and pressed the buttons to start the jets.

6

The next morning, I was up early despite the jetlag, or perhaps because of it. I opened the curtains to take in the panorama of Seoul from my twelfth floor window. It looked like anywhere else in the Western world, a jumble of high rises with a busy eight-lane highway bisecting them. I decided to go out and investigate the

Korean capital up close. I grabbed the abseiling kit and vaulted out of the window. In my dreams.

My first stop was just around the corner: a 600-year-old Confucian complex called the Jongmyo Shrine. After paying the entrance fee, I found myself wandering through a tranquil garden of shrubs and trees. Running through the centre was a stone pathway not meant for mortal tread. The sign read: *Please do not walk on this pathway. This is for the spirits.*

I walked further into the complex and found I wasn't alone. A tour group of Westerners were huddled around a woman who was wearing traditional dress and white gloves. Behind her was a fetching Oriental-looking building with a pointy curved roof.

"This building is the Mangmyoru Pavilion," the guide said. "It is where the king rested before he performed his rituals." She went on to describe a whole load of other things, but I zoned her voice out and began to walk away. Then she shouted at me. "You must stay with us," she admonished. All her flock were looking at me. One man even took a photo. "No wandering off, please."

I was about to argue the toss, but thought, what the hell. I hadn't paid for a guide, but she clearly thought I had, and so I dutifully joined the group, even though I was now marked as a maverick. A few people glanced my way, but most turned back to the guide, who was leading us further into the complex.

The Jeongjeon Hall was massive. It stretched along one side of a wide courtyard and, like the other pavilion, was made of wood and featured a markedly Oriental roof that tapered upwards at each corner. The guide started speaking. "Each of the nineteen rooms inside the hall was for the spirits of the Joseon Dynasty. According to Korean tradition, when a ruler died (or anyone else for that matter), the spirit lived on for four generations. Even though these spirits were invisible, their relatives treated them as part of the family – giving them food, speaking to them, burning incense near their Spirit Tablets and—"

"Excuse me," said a portly gentleman with a walrus moustache. "What are these Spirit Tablets you talk of?" His accent sounded Scandinavian.

"Spirit Tablets are engraved pieces of stone. They have the dead persons' names on them."

The man nodded and rubbed his chin thoughtfully.

7

With the tour over, I wandered along a busy street until I came to another complex belonging to the old Joseon Dynasty: the royal residence of their princes, no less. The almost unpronounceable Changdeokgung was much larger and much more popular that the shrine I'd just visited. In fact, there were hundreds of people wandering around, some with guides.

Even though the Changdeokgung complex looked historically traditional, it was actually quite new. The Japanese were to blame. For six terrible years at the end of the sixteenth century, their mission to conquer Korea and destroy every culturally important building they came across was almost at an end. Their efforts were doomed to failure, largely because China had stepped in to assist the Koreans. Even so, a million people had already lost their lives and then, in their angry retreat, the Japanese attacked the twelfth century Changdeokgung palace, leaving it broken and derelict, a state it remained in for the next two hundred years. Thankfully, someone rebuilt the complex, though with impeccably bad timing. The grand opening coincided with a second Japanese invasion in 1910. By the time the Japanese were thrown out again, following their defeat at the end of the Second World War, only about 30% of the palace complex remained. All of which meant that the palace I was now staring at was less than seventy years old, repaired and restored in the post-war years.

I noticed a large throng of teenage girls loosely following their teacher. The girls were aged about fourteen or fifteen, and instead of studying the ornate walls or the pristine gardens that featured sculptures of dragons and phoenixes, they were more interested in me. Two rushed up, completely unabashed.

"Where you from?" one asked.

"England," I muttered, taken aback by their boldness.

This brought about a giddy explosion of conversation, which brought two more girls over. Then two more. Soon a gaggle of teenage girls surrounded me. So this is how members of One Direction felt. It was actually quite unnerving.

"What your favourite pizza?" another girl asked. Her friend was videotaping me on a small camcorder.

"What your favourite colour?" a different teenager asked, before I had a chance to answer the question.

"Do you prefer Coca Cola or 7-Up?" a third girl asked. The questions were coming thick and fast.

I told her Coca Cola, which brought about an equal measure of nodding and giggling.

"You like Coca Cola? What about Pepsi?"

"Can I take photo?" a tall girl asked, cutting to the chase.

I don't know why she had bothered asking, because her camera was already clicking away. Most of the other girls were doing the same thing. A male voice sounded from somewhere, their teacher, I presumed. The girls scattered and returned to look at a small pond near a pagoda. I made my escape. I decided I'd seen enough temples for the time being and went to find something to eat.

8

I found a fast food restaurant not far from the palace. It was popular with young professionals, most of whom sat chomping away with chopsticks and fast conversation. Not able to read the menu, I pointed to a picture that looked vaguely edible, ordered it, grabbed a spoon from the rack and found a spare table. When the waiter deposited my meal on my table ten minutes later, he told me it was *gamjatang*. Before I had the opportunity to question him further, he was gone.

I regarded my meal. Thankfully, it looked okay. Instead of fish guts and boiled duck beaks, it consisted of potato lumps and chunks of pork, all drowning in a sea of spicy broth. It tasted great and my mood was further buoyed when I discovered the restaurant offered free Wi-Fi. It meant I could check my emails.

The one I wanted to look at was from a tour company. The next day I was planning to visit the Demilitarized Zone near the North Korean border and an email had popped up from them confirming that the trip was still on. This was good news. Relations between the two Koreas were sometimes fraught, meaning tours could be cancelled at any time.

The message also reminded me about wearing the correct clothing. I studied the approved list again: jeans were okay, as long as they didn't have any rips or camouflage markings. T-shirts were fine too, as long as they had a collar and no flags on them. Shorts were not allowed under any circumstances, and neither were skirts or sandals. Any military-looking clothing or cargo pants would mean an automatic jail sentence, and bringing a child under twelve would mean a swift execution. It all sounded very serious and made me even more excited to go.

I finished my pork and potato broth, looked at my watch and decided to see the changing of the guard around the corner.

9

The mother lode of the palaces in Seoul is Gyeonbokgung, the residence of the former royal kings and queens. When I arrived, plenty of people were gathering in a large courtyard guarded by a massive gateway at one end. It was so expansive and beautiful that it could have been a palace itself. Opposite, another huge stone gateway, made up of three mighty arches, backed onto a busy street. Beyond it was modern Seoul.

I turned to look at the main gate. It was gigantic, featuring a double-tiered roof, held up by sturdy columns. Behind it was the palace itself, which looked almost the same as the gateway, except it had some steps leading to its base. With time to spare before the changing of the guard ceremony began, I strode under the gateway and rushed up to the palace. Like many temples, the interior was less impressive than the exterior, as if the designers had built their masterpieces to impress visitors rather than the people who lived in them. Instead of opulent grandeur, the main room was bare, with only a large throne in the middle offering any interest. I returned to where I'd started. There were now hundreds of people.

A woman's voice was giving instructions over a large public address system. We all had to stand behind the blue-taped barrier, she said. While we did so, a man in a bright red frock, tied together with a blue sash around the waist, came into view. On his head he wore a black, wide brimmed hat with a couple of long feathers protruding from the top. He looked like an Alpine Ninja Master. We all regarded him as he stopped near a large upright drum. And there he stood, silent and still, eyes fixed forward.

At the stroke of the hour, he finally moved. First, he banged his drum, which reverberated around the courtyard deeply and ominously; then he bowed and stood still again. With his job done, it was the turn of the musicians, who filtered through a hidden archway, all dressed in similar costumes. Some were playing thin horns, others had drums, a couple of men had cymbals and one had a conch shell. They were playing a tune that fitted the occasion well: it sounded like the soundtrack to *Shogun: March of the Shinju Warriors*. Except the backdrop behind the palace walls was of glass skyscrapers and large plasma TVs telling us the latest currency rates and market movements. The juxtaposition was jarring.

As the musicians played, a new set of men appeared from the large gate. All were dressed in blues, reds, yellows or turquoises. Unlike the musicians, they sported fake moustaches and beards, and carried shields emblazoned with fearsome dragons. In their hands were pikes and strange swords; others had long poles with colourful flags rippling in the breeze. Each man wore strange fabric shoes, black and curved at the end. They looked like oversized elf slippers. After marching around for a short while, they all stopped and the man with the conch shell took centre stage.

He raised the conch to his lips and blew like there was no tomorrow. The sound rang out, echoing across the cobbles and stone walls, growing in intensity before suddenly stopping. Everyone was still, with only the sound of rippling flags or zoom lenses whirring to get a closer shot. Then the musicians started up again and everyone marched back to the gate. The ceremony was over. It was time to leave

10

On the other side of the stone gateway was the traffic of downtown Seoul. It zoomed along, with neither beeps nor angry gestures, but I walked through the centre of it, along a central, pedestrian-only plaza busy with colourful flowerbeds, fountains and stately columns. After a few minutes, I stopped at a massive statue of a seated and smiling man. He was Sejong the Great, the fourth king of the Joseon Dynasty.

How Sejong ascended to the throne is interesting. Born in 1397, he was the third son of the king. As a child, he studied hard, but was always playing third fiddle to his elder brothers, especially Yangnyeong, the eldest of the three princes. As hot favourite to claim the top spot when the king died, palace courtiers groomed Yangnyeong in kingly ways, but it all fell apart when he turned into a typically wayward teenager. Being obnoxiously rude was his new favourite pastime, but some historians have put forward the theory that this behaviour was a ruse. Yangnyeong, they claim, did not wish to be king, and so acted the fool in order for his father to deem him unfit. The final straw came when he married a peasant girl. The king banished him from Seoul, and the prince spent the rest of his days wandering the mountains.

This left the second son, a young man called Hyo-Ryung. He didn't fancy being king either, but instead of taking drastic action as his elder brother had, he simply became a monk and joined a monastery. So all of this meant that Sejong became king at the tender age of twenty-one.

Despite his tender age, Sejong transformed Korea. He abandoned the old ways of government, whereby only the upper class could hold office, and appointed people on merit. As a staunch supporter of Confucianism, he advocated the principle of family harmony. He wrote books about it and the upshot was that Confucianism became part of everyday life in Korea. He eventually died aged 52, due to diabetes. But his statue looked good, and so did his portrait on the 10,000-won note.

Further along the plaza was another statue, this one of a naval commander standing atop a tall plinth. His name was Yi Sun-sin, a charismatic warrior so skilled in the art of sea warfare that he never once lost a battle. This fact is remarkable because Yi never received any formal military training. His greatest triumph came against the Japanese in 1597 when his fleet of thirteen ships faced 133 Japanese warships, and then won. Because of this, and similar acts of expertise, some naval historians regard him as one of the greatest naval commander of all time, on a par with Horatio Nelson.

I gazed up at the old commander. He looked proud and strong, fearsome but fair. His beard was as sharp as his military skill, unlike the naval commander being talked about further along the plaza.

11

A group of people were standing around a small square listening to a woman sing. Her melody was unaccompanied and mournful. Some observers were holding translucent rectangles of blue plastic attached to white poles. The effect was spectral. A cameraman standing at one end of the square was filming everything.

A few people were holding cardboard portraits of teenagers in school uniforms. One showed the photo of a young woman with long black hair. The message read: *Missing at sea. Please find my daughter Da-Yoon.*

The woman singing, the photos and flags were memorials to hundreds of people who lost their lives in one of South Korea's worst shipping accidents. My visit to Seoul had coincided with the two-year anniversary of this terrible event. On one awful day in April 2014, 250 students from the same high school drowned, together with 101 other passengers. The people gathered in the square were asking questions: *Where is my child? Why did they die? What exactly happened on that dreadful day?*

The causes of the disaster are complex and difficult to discern. But one key fact is that, when the Korean ferry company bought the ship from Japan in 2012, the *Sewel* was already 18 years old, older than most ships worldwide. But the new owners made extensive modifications. For a start, the number of passenger cabins was increased, and the general weight of the ship was made larger. This might have been fine, except for one critical oversight: the Sewel now had a left-right imbalance. It wasn't much of an imbalance but, as we shall see, it would be enough to make all the difference.

And so the good ship Sewel set to work, plying the fourteen-hour route between Incheon and the Korean island of Jeju, a journey which it undertook three times a week. On the day of the accident, the ferry was beginning its 242nd round trip, with a busy passenger manifest that included teenagers from Danwon High School. As they boarded, below them, unseen and unnoticed, was the ship's cargo. Much of it was unsecured, but worse was the weight: it was double the legal limit. The ferry left the port of Incheon and began its journey south.

In charge of the ship that day was a temporary captain. The usual captain had asked for some repairs to be made on the steering gear; he was worried about the imbalance. The ferry company ignored his request. When he pressed them further, they threatened him with dismissal. So for reasons unknown, this man was not in charge of the ship that day.

Most of the journey passed without incident. In the twelfth hour of the voyage, almost at the end of the journey, the Sewel began traversing a channel in the south of the country. At the helm was the third mate, a 25-year-old woman with limited experience in steering large ferries. The captain, not required by law to be at the helm, was in his cabin. He came in to check on her at 8.37am, and stayed for four minutes. The chief engineer also checked in on the third mate, and after observing her carrying out her duties satisfactorily, he too left her to get on with it.

Ten minutes later, the third officer believed they were on a collision course with another ship. She ordered the helmsman to turn the ship by five degrees, the maximum allowed for a ship overloaded with cargo and dangerously top-heavy. With the turn too slow for her liking, and believing a collision imminent, she ordered another five-degree turn. The helmsman, confused by the rapid series of orders, turned the ship by a further ten degrees. It was this second turn that set the disaster in motion.

To turn ten degrees, most ocean-going vessels take around four minutes. The Sewel took one second, causing the ship to tilt twenty degrees in the water. Almost immediately, the unsecured cargo below deck shifted position, tilting the ship by a further ten degrees. The Sewel was now listing dangerously. In panic, the helmsman swung the wheel fifteen degrees the other direction, but, instead of righting the ship, it made things worse. Things deteriorated quickly from then on in.

Water sluiced through the cargo doors and passengers were thrown against bulkheads. In the midst of the burgeoning disaster, the captain somehow made it to the bridge. He arrived just before the chief engineer, who immediately shut down the engines. In the corner was the third officer, weeping. Then the lights went out.

The time was 8.52am, only four minutes into the disaster. Soon after, the crew made a passenger announcement over the in-house speaker system: *"Do not move. Stay where you are. It's dangerous if you move."* The problem with this order was that water was flooding into passenger cabins. Some passengers ignored the order and ran for the upper reaches of the stricken ship; most did as instructed and stayed put. At around the same time, the first emergency call was made to the outside world; not by the crew, but by a high school student on his mobile phone. He had elected to remain in his room where he would soon drown. The crew inside the bridge made their emergency call three minutes later.

For the next few awful minutes, the Sewel filled with water while emergency vessels rushed to assist. The captain and then the communications officer repeatedly ordered passengers to remain in their cabins but, by 9.30am, they realised things were futile and finally gave the order to evacuate. Unfortunately, this order did not reach most of the passengers, either because the intercom system had failed or it was simply too noisy to hear it. So while the ship's crew started abandoning ship, hundreds of passengers remained in their cabins.

The captain and chief engineer were among the first people to be rescued, even though, according to Korean law, it was illegal for a ship's captain to abandon ship if there are still passengers aboard. The ferry took two and a half hours to sink. The last text message sent by a passenger trapped inside was at 10.17am, then all communications ceased. Three hundred and fifty one people drowned. When the world woke up on 17th April 2014, shock rang out. As families mourned their loss, and a high school faced the horror of losing most of its older students, the captain was arrested with the helmsman and female third officer. At the same time, the vice principal of the high school, who had been aboard the ship but had been rescued, hanged himself. His suicide note read, 'I might be a teacher in heaven to those kids'.

More arrests followed. Then police charged the captain and chief engineer with homicide. The helmsman and third officer faced the lesser charge of abandoning a ship. The chairman of the ferry company went into hiding. His body was found a few months later, his death most probably caused by suicide. By November, the first court cases were being held in Seoul. Captain Lee Jin-seok was sentenced to spend the rest of his life in prison. The chief engineer got twenty years; the weeping third mate got ten. Thirteen other crew members received prison sentences of up to twelve years. Today, nine bodies remain missing.

13

Back in the centre of the city, I descended into Seoul's subterranean world of escalators, tunnels and subway trains. It was easy to navigate and I was soon sitting aboard a train to Daebang Station. All of my fellow passengers were Korean, every one of them staring into mobile phones. I wasn't; I was staring at the notice in the upper portion of the window opposite. It had a set of graphics showing the rules of conduct aboard the train. Some were ordinary, such as not shouting into mobile phones, not throwing bags around the cabin and not swinging from the hand holders dangling from the ceiling. Not eating burgers seemed a reasonable request too, as did the rule advising people not to lie down and fall asleep, thereby rendering an entire seating section useless. The graphic depicting a person vomiting made me smile, as did the one of someone shaking a wet umbrella. But the oddest one showed a man sitting with his knees wide apart. Was this frowned upon in Korean society, I wondered? I looked down and closed my legs.

Twenty minutes later, I alighted from a tube station on the south of the River Han. After negotiating the barriers, I emerged into the evening sunlight. My destination was a tall, golden skyscraper called 63 Building, named because of the number of floors it had. I was only interested in one of them, though: the 60th. It was home to an observation deck.

Soon I was up there, looking down upon the sprawl of Seoul. Skyscrapers, lines of residential blocks lined up like white Lego, looping highways, meandering railway lines and, of course, the river, snaking through it all, were all behind the glass windows. It was a fitting way to end my day of sightseeing in the high-tech South Korean capital. As the sun went down, casting a pinkish hue over the horizon, I thought it remarkable how a city over two thousand years old could look so modern.

An hour later, I descended inside the safety of an elevator. It was time to head back to the hotel; I needed an early night. The next day, I was heading north to visit a strip of land that separated two nations at war. The Korean Demilitarized Zone (or DMZ) was the most heavily armed piece of real estate on the planet and I was going to be standing in the middle of it.

Clockwise from top left: Downtown Seoul has some great architecture; Changing of the guard ceremony at Gyeonbokgung, the former royal residence; If anyone ever fancies abseiling from a hotel window in Seoul, then this kit will come in handy; Sejong the Great, the fourth king of the Joseon Dynasty; Neon signs in downtown Seoul; The main temple of Gyeonbokgung

Chapter 12: A Day trip to the Demilitarized Zone

I awoke excited. The trip to the border with North Korea promised intrigue and probable drama. There was even a remote possibility shots would be fired.

I read the itinerary provided by the tour company again. It said the eight-hour trip would include a visit to the War Memorial of Korea, then somewhere called Camp Bonifas, where we would watch a presentation and sign some forms. After that, we would drive to the main attraction, the JSA: the Joint Security Area, where soldiers from both Koreas stood face-to face (so to speak) in a demilitarized zone. As well as witnessing this strange standoff, we would be able to walk inside a large room split between both nations. So for a few seconds, I would actually be able to stand in North Korea.

The only problem with the tour was the tour itself. I loathed organised excursion companies. Sitting on a bus with a whole crowd of strangers while someone herded us around the sights was my idea of hell. But since it was the only way to visit the DMZ, I had to put up with it. I grabbed a quick cup of coffee and then headed outside. It was 8am and the people of Seoul were on their way to work, all suited and booted, not a button or smudge out of place. The jewellery sellers were open for business, as were the chophouses. Mr Watch was sitting there, too, his hands still thrust deep inside his pockets. Buses, cars and a steady stream of taxis paraded along the main routes. I bypassed the masses, following a map to the Lotte Hotel.

I found it along the next street. The Lotte Hotel was a luxury establishment towering over a busy intersection. The tour company's office was on the sixth floor, home to a whole raft of similar tour companies. I was early and the first person there. After introducing myself, the woman behind the desk checked I had my passport and then gave my clothes the once over. I was worried actually. My jeans had some small rips in them, which I'd read were not allowed. The woman didn't say anything and so I pointed them out to her. She said they were fine. 77,000 won later (£53), the deal was done.

"Wait in car park for bus like this." She showed me a photo of a large red silver bus. "It come at nine. Enjoy trip."

Because it was only half past eight, I decided to have a walk around outside. It was chilly but bearable, and I strained my neck to look up at the skyscrapers around me. If not for the green road signs splashed with Korean, and the Asian faces on the street with me, I could have been in New York, Sydney or Berlin. I walked as far as the next intersection before turning back; I didn't want to be late.

The bus arrived at the allotted time and a whole pack of people climbed aboard. We all had allocated seating and the bus was almost full. Being one of only two single passengers, I had the one spare seat next to me. The other solo passenger was a prematurely balding man further back. Opposite me was an actor from the hit TV series, *Lost*. The large man looked identical to Hurley, the longhaired and portly character from the program. When I heard him speaking to his companion with an American accent, I began to think it might actually be him. With a long journey ahead of us, I had plenty of time to find out for sure. But for now, as excited chatter filled the interior, I waited for the tour to begin.

2

A Korean woman climbed aboard. She stood at the front and picked up a small microphone. She was in her late thirties and, after a few crackles and squeaks, she began speaking.

"So welcome to the tour. My name is Gayeong, and the driver is called Yehoon. Is everyone okay?"

There were a few murmured replies to this, but most people remained quiet. It was too early and too sombre an occasion for trivialities.

"Well, our first stop will be the War Memorial of Korea, which is about ten minutes away, depending on traffic. There you will see the cause of the conflict with our Northern neighbour, and can see many exhibits. After the museum, we will drive north to the border. That will take about one hour. Just before we get there, we will stop for lunch. So can I ask whether anyone is vegetarian?"

No one said anything.

The woman smiled. "That makes it easy. After lunch, we will proceed to the Demilitarized Zone. Before that, I will give you some important information. But for now, sit back, relax and enjoy the tour."

The driver started the engine and the tour began.

Eleven minutes later (I checked), we pulled up in a large car park full of other coaches. Outside was a huge 33-foot statue of two soldiers hugging: one from South Korea, the other North Korea. The *Two Brothers* represented a pair of Korean siblings meeting in the midst of battle: a symbol of hope that, one day, North and South Korea may unite.

Outside the entrance of the sombre grey museum, Gayeong gathered us together. I surreptitiously moved closer to Hurley, in the hope of hearing him discussing acting or plotlines from *Lost* with his companion, but he was silent, staring at the engraved names of the dead. The vast majority were Koreans (from both sides), numbering over a quarter of a million. China came in third place, with hundreds of thousands of men dead, with USA fourth (36,575 deaths). There were plenty of other countries too, including the UK (1,109), Australia (339), Ethiopia (121), Philippines (92), and even Luxembourg with 2 casualties. The list of names was mammoth and impossible to read individually. But as a graphic depiction of those killed in the three-year conflict, it was highly effective.

"You will have forty-five minutes to see the exhibits, inside and outside the museum," Gayeong told us. "And then we will meet in the car park at 9.50. Is this okay?" I was already leaving the herd, forging forwards into the large building.

As I was largely ignorant of the Korean War, the museum turned out to be interesting. Photos, grainy black-and-white film, endless artefacts and paintings all gave me a flavour of what happened.

3

The root cause was the Second World War. As the two advancing armies of America and the Soviet Union squeezed the Japanese into submission, they made an agreement. The Soviets would push as far south as the 38th parallel, a line of latitude that more or less split the landmass of Korea in two; the Americans would push northwards and stop at the same line. Then, when Japan surrendered, they would decide what to do. This settled, the armies pushed forward.

On 8th September 1945, Japan surrendered, leaving Korea in the hands of the Soviets and the Americans. The Soviets controlled the North, the Americans controlled the South. But because both sides could not trust one another, the postwar years proved to be a period of tension and unease.

By 1948, things took a turn for the worse when the Americans held elections in their southern portion, which led to the establishment of the Republic of Korea. The Russians refused to acknowledge it and, in defiance, backed the formation of the Democratic People's Republic of Korea in the North, installing Kim Il-sung, grandfather of the current supreme leader, Kin Jongun, in charge. With a choice of communism or democracy, people began to move from North to South and vice versa. Then movement was stopped. And with this tense standoff, the Americans and Soviets decided to withdraw. The Koreas were on their own to sort out the mess.

To fill the power vacuum, China came into the game, flooding North Korea with weapons. With this backing, North Korea prepared itself to invade the South, believing that America would sit idly by. And so, in June 1950, before the sun had even began to make its way above the Eastern horizon, the first North Korean troops crossed the

38th parallel with heavy artillery and tanks. The South Koreans were utterly overwhelmed and unprepared and, in the face of such a well-planned assault, couldn't do a thing. Jubilant, the North Korean war machine marched towards Seoul and the South Korean president was evacuated. In just five days, seventy thousand South Korean soldiers were dead.

But the United States did not stand idly by. They sent in troops, and plenty of them, together with a whole raft of ships and aircraft. By September 1950, they had reclaimed Seoul and had begun a push northward. As they approached the 38th parallel, China warned the Americans that, if they crossed it, they would join the war on the side of the North Koreans. When US troops crossed the parallel, China made good their threat. And so the battle raged on, with attacks and counterattacks, but little movement of actual territory for either side. It was a war of attrition that killed thousands.

By July 1953, three years on from the initial invasion, all parties signed an armistice, effectively ending the war. Three quarters of a million people lay dead with nothing achieved except a piece of paper saying both sides had to stick to the area they already held back in 1950. To keep the sides separate, a 2.5-milewide strip of land called the Korean Demilitarized Zone came into being, running along the 38th parallel for its entire 160 miles. The only official place where both countries could meet was in a Joint Security Area at the Western end.

In the years since the armistice, South Korea has become an Asian success story, affording its people an excellent standard of life and making its capital one of the most modern in the world. Conversely, the North, run by an increasingly unstable government in Pyongyang, has become a paranoid pariah state, where many of its population scrabble around to make ends meet. Both sides meet occasionally to ratify a few agreements and such like, but mostly they just stare at one another through binoculars.

I wandered outside to see some military hardware, including jet fighters, large transport aircraft, helicopters, tanks and a replica of a ship peppered with bullet holes that the North Koreans sank in 2002. The exhibits covered a huge area, and there was nowhere near enough time to see them all.

Instead, I wandered over to another great statue, this one showing soldiers in the midst of battle. As a young boy, I avidly read *Commando* comics, thinking that war was exciting. Being part of a platoon, heading deep into enemy territory, battling with your friends by your side, sounded like prime adventure and fun. Aged ten, I had been fooled by these romantic notions of war, where fellow comrades said things like, 'toodle-oo' and 'tally-ho' and always returned to base for a cup of tea. At the time, I had wanted to be in the army, or the air force (never the navy for some reason), but now I couldn't think of anything worse; battling enemies who used to be brothers and cousins, being blown up or taken prisoner to be tortured and buried in an unmarked grave: there was nothing remotely romantic about it.

By chance, Hurley from Lost came over to the statue. He and his pal were laughing about something that had happened the previous evening. From what I could gather, they had been out drinking, when one of them had fallen over, or something. Feeling bold, I decided to introduce myself.

"Hi," I said, sticking my hand out. "I'm Jason. I think we're on the same tour."

"Hi," said Hurley, shaking my hand. His friends shook my hand too. "Yeah, I think I recognise you from the coach. You're sitting across the aisle, right?"

Neither presented their names, and I couldn't ask them outright, not without sounding like a fruitcake, so I simply offered a few observations about the trip and about how much I was looking forward to seeing the Demilitarized Zone. They nodded and murmured agreement. When they started taking photos, I shuffled my feet for a bit and then left them alone. It was time to head back to the bus, anyway.

5

As we trundled northward, Gayeong picked up her microphone. "If you look to your left, you will see North Korea on the other side of the river."

Everyone stared outside past the road upon which we were travelling. The river looked swollen and heavy from rain the previous week and, beyond it, North Korea looked barren and empty. Instead of buildings and modern highways, it was countryside and small hills. At the side of the road was a long barbed wire fence dotted with the occasional camouflaged guard tower. It was an ominous sign of what was to come. Traffic was light. After all, who but tourists and military personnel would be travelling this way?

Gayeong spoke again. "Many people ask whether anyone has ever defected across the Demilitarized Zone. Well let me say this: the answer is yes. In 1984, a man from the Soviet Union who was part of a tour from the North – yes, North Korea also provides tours of the Demilitarized Zone – left his tour group and ran south across the border. Some North Korean soldiers chased him with weapons, but the Americans and South Koreans chased them back. Even so, four soldiers died, one from South Korea and three from the North. As for the Soviet defector, he was saved and I think he ended up in California."

We stopped at the Imjingak Peace Park, seven kilometres from the Demilitarized Zone, named after the Imjin River, which meandered around the west of the complex. As well as its monuments, observation deck and flags, the peace park was home to a sorry-looking fairground and a large restaurant catering for tourists. The latter had the potential to be the most stressful aspect of the whole trip for me: as a solo traveller, eating alone did not promise much merriment.

Our guide led us upstairs into a dining area. "Okay," Gayeong said chirpily, "Please find a seat at one of these tables and your food will be brought out. You have thirty-five minutes for lunch."

I waited while the groups and couples took their seats. When everyone had, I surveyed the remaining places. There was a space on a table of eight and a space on a table of four. The actor from Lost was sitting at the larger table. I opted for the smaller table of four. Already seated were a young couple and a slightly older man, the prematurely balding individual I had noticed on the coach. All three were Westerners.

The couple, Craig and Jenna, were from Huddersfield, not far from where I lived. The man was from Hamburg, Germany, and his name was Franz. Offering his name was the final conversation piece he offered to the table, preferring instead to read his guidebook. I had planned on doing something similar, but ended up chatting to the young couple from Yorkshire.

They told me they lived in Hong Kong where they worked as teachers. "The kids are great," said Jenna, "but the pay's not too good. Most of our money goes on our tiny one-bedroom apartment."

I asked them how long they had been in South Korea.

"Two days. Then, tomorrow, we're flying to Tokyo." As the German stuffed his mouth with noodles and chicken, Craig explained that they were trying to see as much of the Far East as possible before finishing their two-year teaching contract.

I smiled. "Make sure you try the toilets in Tokyo."

"The toilets?" Jenna asked. The German raised his eyes.

"They're all space age and electronic. They're great. Mind you, my room in Seoul has one too."

The German excused himself and left the table, probably to visit the observation deck, or maybe to find a toilet. We had all tried engaging him in talk, but either his English wasn't up to conversation or he simply didn't want to talk. Either way, he was gone now, and so I decided to point out the actor from Lost to the couple from Huddersfield. They both looked. Jenna turned back to me. "Oh my God!"

I nodded, smiling. "I know."

"Do you think it's him?"

I shrugged. Craig found some Wi-Fi and Googled him. He told me that an actor called Jorge Garcia had played the part of Hurley. There was a photo of him. We compared the photo to the man across from us. The actor looked older, but not by much. Our man also seemed thinner, but that didn't prove a thing. We were none the wiser.

I decided to follow the German up to the observation deck. I waved goodbye to Craig and Jenna and promised to tell them if I found out any more information about the famous actor who might be in our midst.

6

The observation deck offered a panorama of the river and the Demilitarised Zone beyond. North Korea was about four kilometres away as the crow flies. Although the zone looked barren and devoid of human settlement, I knew this was not the case. Both Koreas kept 'peace' villages. I couldn't see either from my vantage point, but I knew that the settlements were out there somewhere, only a mile distant from each another. Both featured gigantic national flags. The South Koreans built their flag first, proud of its impressive 323-feet height. The North Koreans placed their flag soon after. It was two hundred feet taller.

The South Korean peace village is called Daeseong-Dong, home to about 250 people, mostly farmers. The South Korean government pays them handsomely for their work and, unlike the rest of the South Korean population, exempts them from paying tax. The downside is that they are living in a potential warzone and they have to put up with propaganda blaring out from gigantic speakers.

Between 2004 and 2015, the speakers were silent. Then, following North Korea's testing of nuclear weapons, they powered them up again. From the south, the propaganda extols the virtues of living in a democratic nation, hoping that any North Korean listening will defect. They also send news reports describing how well South Korea is doing, while at the same time pointing out the corruption of the North. Occasionally, the speakers blast out South Korean pop music, just to annoy the North. Pop music is banned in North Korea.

The propaganda coming in from the North simply condemns the South and its allies. They lambast every aspect of life in South Korea, hoping that someone will make a run for it and embrace their way of life. Both sides blast out messages for up to six hours per day, often in the middle of the night.

Because the South Korea speaker system is more advanced than its northerly neighbour's, the North Koreans have threatened to blow the speakers up. And even though this state of play seems almost childish, for the people of Daeseong-Dong, and Kijong-dong in the North, living in a 'peace' village must be anything but.

Back at ground level, I wandered towards a hulking, rusting, brown, bullet-ridden mess that was once a train. During the war, the old coal-powered locomotive had transported American and South Korean troops to the front lines. But on New Year's Eve, 1950, as the train was reversing to the South to collect more men and ammunition, US troops attacked it. North Korean troops had been using it as a free ride to the South and the Americans wanted to put an end to it once and for all. For almost six decades, the train was left to rust and fall apart on its forgotten tracks until the South Korean authorities put it on a truck, did some restoration work and deposited it inside the Imjingak complex. I wandered around the train, listening to the strange music being piped in from somewhere. It sounded like a mixture of jazz and mournful Korean pop. Perhaps it was propaganda. Whatever it was, it sounded dreadful.

"He's not Hurley," said Craig from Huddersfield, who had found me loitering near the coach.

Jenna was with him. "We managed to sneak a look at his passport. His name's Roland Poole."

I nodded. "Makes sense. I doubt a famous actor would slum it on a tour like ours. He'd organise his own private one. I know I would."

We all climbed on the bus, including the man now identified as Roland Poole. I found my seat and prepared myself for the main objective of the tour. At the front, Gayeong picked up the microphone.

"Okay, this is the serious part of the tour." Her voice was appropriately sombre. "In a few minutes we will drive to the Unification Bridge. There are barricades there, but everything is perfectly safe. Our driver will stop the coach and a soldier will come aboard and count us. Another soldier will check your passports."

We all digested this information in silence.

"After that, we will proceed to Camp Bonifas, a United Nations outpost. There is a theatre there where we will watch a short presentation." She paused, waiting until she had everyone's full attention. "And one last thing: from now on, we are entering a sensitive military area and therefore please do not take any photos, unless directed to do so by me or the military guide, who you will meet later. If you are caught taking a photo or trying to film in an unauthorised location, then it will be a very serious matter. Not just for you, but for all of us, especially me."

The coach was deathly silent. Then the engine started and we began to drive towards North Korea. Along the way, I caught sight of the gigantic flagpole that belonged to the North. That's how close we were.

Manning Camp Bonifas are a few hundred South Korean and American military personnel. Triple coils of barbed wire surround its perimeter. As well as being battle-ready, the soldiers stationed at Camp Bonifas act as guides for the eight hundred or so tourists who visit most days. When the soldiers are not doing official duties, they can relax by taking their clubs onto the most dangerous golf course in the world. If a ball goes astray, there's a good chance it will land on a landmine. Camp Bonifas is surrounded by mines.

The coach passed under a large sign that announced we were entering the United Nations Command Security Battalion Joint Security Area. To our right was a field, busy with troops. They were practising with rifles. A set of targets was at the far end. When our coach stopped a little further in, a young man in uniform approached. He climbed onto the bus and walked along the aisle counting us. Everyone was silent. Then he returned to the front.

"Welcome to the Joint Security Area," he said in a clipped American, no-nonsense tone. "I'll be your guide from here on in, and my first job is to check your passports."

Gayeong started collecting them as we followed the soldier off the coach. Outside, we assembled in front of the corporal. He looked young – but hard as nails. While we waited, he began checking through everyone's passport. Specifically, he was looking for anyone from Afghanistan, Cuba, Iran, Iraq, Libya, Pakistan, Sudan, Syria or North Korea, all of whom would be barred from proceeding any further. When he was satisfied that none of us were on the banned list, he looked up. "I'm going to ask a question, and I want you all to listen carefully." We all waited. He narrowed his eyes and then said, "Are any of you thinking of defecting today?"

There were a few titters and some chortles. The American soldier wasn't laughing, though; he was looking at each of us in turn. When nobody tried to make a run for it, he nodded. "Good. Let's continue."

He led us towards a large, modern building that turned out to be the DMZ visitor's centre. Inside, there was a large auditorium with a cinema screen at the front. A few other tour groups were already there. For the next twenty minutes, we all watched a series of slides and movie clips about the conflict and history of the Joint Security Area. The most interesting segment was about the axe murders.

It all started because of a tree.

9

The tree in question was a tall poplar tree that just happened to be in the way of things. It blocked one UN checkpoint's line of sight to another UN checkpoint. This second checkpoint was close to the infamous Bridge of No Return, the point where prisoners of war could cross between the Koreas but, like its name suggested, never return. The lonely checkpoint was the closest piece of protected UN land to the North Korean border.

As the poplar tree's branches grew and became ever bushier, the North Koreans realised something. Theoretically, they could rush over the short wooden bridge, grab some UN personnel and take them to North Korea without anyone noticing. They decided to try.

Unfortunately, they never managed to snatch anyone. Each of their kidnap attempts ended in failure, but they did annoy the United Nations troops who had to deal with them. Things heated up further when a group of armed North Korean soldiers stormed the unseen checkpoint and held some American troops hostage. It wasn't a kidnap attempt, merely a show of strength. They departed soon after, leaving the UN soldiers annoyed and embarrassed.

So something had to be done about the damned tree.

On a warm day on 18 August 1976, a group of Korean and US soldiers went to chop it down. Two of the Americans were Captain Arthur Bonifas and First Lieutenant Mark Barret. Bonifas was a handsome, thirty-three-year old father of three and husband to Marcia. As his party of tree choppers drove out to the poplar tree, he was looking forward to seeing his family again when he flew home a few days later. His second-in-command, Lieutenant Barret was younger, aged only 25. He was married to Julianne and, like his commanding officer, was due to fly home in the near future.

As the group climbed from their truck to inspect the poplar tree, a group of North Korean soldiers walked across the Bridge of No Return and started watching them. Undeterred, the tree trimming party began pruning some branches, and did so for the next fifteen minutes. Suddenly, the commander of the North Korean troops ordered them to stop, saying that Kim Jong-Il, the Supreme Leader, had personally planted the tree in his youth. It was an unlikely story, and one Captain Bonifas didn't believe. He ordered that the pruning continue.

The North Korean commander, angry at the slight, said something to one of his underlings, who then ran back across the bridge. While leaves and branches fell to the ground, a truck carrying North Korean reinforcements came trundling over the bridge. With this show of force, the North Korean commander ordered the tree clipping gang to desist again. Captain Bonifas told his men to carry on, which set the scene for what was to follow.

Witnesses claim the North Korean commander calmly removed his watch and put it in his pocket. Then, after watching the tree being trimmed further, he gave an order to attack the two American officers. Before Captain Bonifas could react, a group of North Koreans fell upon him with axes and clubs, killing him there and them. Lieutenant Barret escaped over a nearby wall, pursued by other North Korean troops. Meanwhile, under the tree, a sizeable group of North Koreans began to attack the pruning party. Only the quick-thinking of the truck driver, who drove his vehicle into the melee, stopped more deaths. While everyone ran for it, and the North Koreans retreated, Lieutenant Barret lay bleeding and cut. He died soon after.

Things happened quickly after that. In an attempt to create confusion, North Korea announced to the world that imperialist aggressors armed with axes had just committed an unprovoked attack on some of their guards. The American officers' deaths were due to self-defence, they claimed. Kim Jon-il demanded that US forces withdraw from Korea immediately. In Washington, President Gerald Ford and his advisors held an emergency meeting. They quickly decided not to withdraw and instead to do the opposite.

Three days later, they took action. Sixteen military engineers in possession of chainsaws and axes headed towards the tree. With them were 800 troops armed with guns, grenades and rocket launchers. It was a ridiculous show of force, but its purpose was to intimidate the North Koreans into submission. If the ground troops didn't do the trick, then maybe the swarms of Cobra helicopters and fighter jets streaking through the sky above them would.

At the poplar tree, which had started the whole thing, the first truck arrived in place. Across the border, North Korean binoculars twitched in consternation. When an American military engineer climbed onto the roof of the truck and started chopping at branches, everyone waited for North Korea's response. When nothing happened, other engineers started chopping too. Forty minutes later, only a large stump remained.

Then something unusual occurred. Kim Jung-il sent a message to the United Nations, expressing 'regret' for the earlier incident. It wasn't an apology, but it was as close to one as they would get. Soon after, the UN renamed the place Camp Bonifas, and they replaced the tree stump with a brass monument. Bonifas and Barret were posthumously awarded Purple Heart medals.

10

When the show ended, our guide stood at the front of the auditorium. She was holding a pile of paper in her hands. "Please listen, everyone. These are Visitor Declaration Forms. All of you are required to read and sign one. She began to pass them around. When I got mine, I read it carefully. The printed A4 piece of paper explained the rules and regulations of our visit. *The visit to the Joint Security Area at Panmunjom will entail the entrance into a hostile area and the possibility of injury or death as a direct result of enemy action.* It went on to state: *The United States of America and the Republic of Korea cannot guarantee the safety of visitors and may not be held accountable in the event of a hostile enemy act.* It was all very sobering and highlighted how serious the situation was.

The rest of the sheet spelled out the rules. We should not point, gesture, or make scoffing sounds that could be misconstrued as aggressive acts. Everyone should also follow the orders of their guide throughout the visit. Anybody who had consumed alcohol in the last twelve hours would be banned from the tour. I signed and dated the bottom of the sheet, my life now in the hands of military personnel and their whims.

Before the next portion of the tour began, our guide stood at the front once again. Other guides were doing the same thing. She told us that we would be boarding military coaches. "Please listen to the military guide who will go with you. Follow their orders and do not take any photos unless directed to do so. Afterwards, when you arrive back here, please find our coach and sit and wait. You will know our coach because it is grey and red and has 'A' written on the front. Do not go to the 'B' bus. I will now collect the forms."

We all handed over the signed forms, went outside and boarded a military coach, which was just the same as our other one, except older. We drove a short distance and stopped. It was now time for the real part of the tour to begin. My excitement level turned up a notch.

11

"Everybody line up two abreast," commanded the American corporal assigned to us, the same man who had checked our passports. "We are going to enter the building behind me. When we do, we'll climb some stairs. Please walk in an orderly fashion, following me, until we arrive at some doors that lead outside. Opposite you will be North Korea. Once we're out, I will take you to a place where we will stop. As we walk there, do not look left or right. Keep your eyes fixed to the front. Until we get there, I don't want any talking or anyone taking pictures. Let's go."

The last time I'd walked in silent formation was at school. Probably the same for everyone else. The Hurley lookalike was just in front of me, as were the couple from Huddersfield. Because the German guy was a solo traveller, he stood alongside me. We nodded at each other but kept silent as we climbed the staircase. My excitement level was now even higher. The situation was tense, made more so by the tone of the corporal, coupled with the form I had just signed.

At the top of the stairs, we marched in silence towards some open doors. Sunlight streamed in. When he led us outside, we all gawped at North Korea. It was mostly trees and hidden structures, apart from a single three-storey building opposite. We didn't get a chance to study it in detail because our guide was leading us along the front of the long UN building. After a few metres, he stopped and so did we, still in our pairs.

"As I speak to you right now," he said, "you are being monitored by cameras and listening devices. By both sides. So please do not make any gestures or point anywhere. The large grey building over there is called Panmungak; it belongs to North Korea. It was built in 1969 and is only 260 feet away. It is the headquarters of the North Korean guards. In a moment, I'm going to allow you to take some photos of it. There are two rules about this: one, do not move from this area and two, do not take a photo of our UN building, only photos pointing that way." He pointed to North Korea. "Okay, take some photos."

Everyone turned to look at North Korea. I zoomed in on a North Korean soldier standing to attention near the front of the grey building. Wearing a neatly pressed green-uniform and helmet, the young man stood stock still with his hands clenched. Despite this look of pretend aggression, he looked quite friendly. Closer to us, roughly in the centre of the North and South Korean border were a few blue painted huts. A group of South Korean soldiers, all facing the North, stood next to them, hands clenched, legs spaced apart. It was a stance of pure aggression, yet, to me, it looked a little bit silly.

"Okay," said the corporal, "it is our turn in the Conference Building, which is the blue building to the left." We watched as a tour group left, and we started moving to replace them. In turn, a third tour group filled the gap we were leaving. Everything was running like clockwork.

"We have ten minutes inside and you can take photographs of whatever you want, even of the guards. But please do not touch the tables. One last thing, the conference room is split in half: one half belongs to South Korea, the other North Korea. The large table in the middle marks the border. Let's go."

12

We all trooped into the conference room. Occasionally, representatives from both sides met inside this very room, the guide informed us. The room was rectangular and, like the exterior, was painted blue. White tiles covered the floor, with tables and leather chairs neatly arranged upon them. The largest table was in the middle of the room. It had a small UN flag resting at one end and a microphone wire running along its centre. The wire marked the border between North and South Korea. On the other side of the table was North Korea. None of us dared go there because of the guards in the room. Two ridiculously young South Korean soldiers were standing to attention at both ends of the room. One was in the North Korean end. Both had their fists clenched, had a sidearm and wore helmets emblazoned with white Korean lettering. They also sported cool shades.

Gayeong, our original guide from Seoul, was in the room with us. She noticed our reticence at moving across the border. "Listen everyone, please move around in here. Go over to the other side. The guards do not mind."

I walked into North Korea. The guard stood still, only his eyes flickered. He didn't look old enough to shave and yet the mood inside the Conference Building was undoubtedly tense. I walked over to a side window and looked outside. A concrete slab on the ground formed another international border, the most dangerous one in the world. And then our ten minutes was up. We all took a flurry of photos: of the table, of the guards, of us standing with a guard and of us loitering in North Korea. It was easily the best part of the tour. We all returned to the main building from where we came and boarded the military coach for the final part of the visit.

After a few minutes, we stopped but had to remain on the bus. On our right was the brass memorial to the two US soldiers killed by North Korea. It was a small cube with an engraved placard on the top, bearing the names of the two officers who died that fateful day. It marked the place where the poplar tree had once stood. Not far was the infamous Bridge of No Return, now no longer in use. Four sturdy bollards blocked the tiny wooden crossing. And that was it: the end of the tour. Only one more thing to look forward to: embarrassment of the highest order.

13

Back in the main car park, Gayeong led us to the Demilitarized Zone gift shop. If the desire had taken me, I could have bought some North Korean money, a bottle of South Korean wine, a collection of military memorabilia, T-shirts, a map, some books or even a pair of Korean flags. The shop was doing a roaring trade, with people buying all sorts of crap. Tour groups and guides were everywhere. It was ridiculous.

I soon grew bored and retired to the bus, making sure I found exactly the same seat number as before. When more people began to board, I started looking though my photos just as a man took the seat next to me. I thought his presence odd, but perhaps now that the tour was over, passengers could sit where they like, I reasoned. Though why the young man had opted to sit next to me was anyone's guess.

A few more passengers came aboard. A Japanese-looking couple took the seats where Hurley and his friend had been sitting. So it *was* a free-for-all. Soon the bus seemed full and a female guide, not Gayeong wandered along the aisle, counting us all.

"Good tour, eh?" I said to the man next to me.

He nodded. "Loved it." His accent was Australian. "The Conference Room was fantastic."

A microphone crackled into life. "Ah ... hi, everybody. We have a problem. One of the passengers from the other bus is missing."

There was a collective 'aah' aboard the bus. Had someone defected to North Korea? Had someone been kidnapped? The guide wandered along the aisle again, counting heads. When she finished, she counted us a third time. Then she picked up the microphone. "Erm ... we have an extra passenger aboard this bus. I think this passenger is on the wrong bus. If you think it is you, can you please identify yourself?"

The Aussie looked at me.

I looked back at him. He was the missing passenger, quite obviously. The fool had got on the wrong bus.

He said, "I think that's your bus over there, mate."

I dug out my original ticket. It said seat number 14a. I looked up and saw that I was sitting in the correct seat. And then the terrible realisation hit me. I was sitting on the wrong bloody bus. I was causing a scene in a warzone and so I stood up, shuffled past the Australian man and began the Walk of Shame. I then had a second Walk of Shame when I climbed aboard the correct coach. I took my seat a broken man, embarrassed and ashamed. North Korea had claimed another victim. I tried to hide myself in the far reaches of my seat for the entire trip back to Seoul.

14

Back in my hotel room in central Seoul, I grabbed a sandwich from across the street and a couple of bottles of Cass lager from the 7-Eleven before retiring to my room. After drinking one bottle of the supersized 750ml beer, I probably wouldn't be up to abseiling from the window, but drank it anyway, and didn't care. As I packed my bags for another flight, I mulled over my trip to South Korea. It had been better than expected, full of history, tension and a fair dollop of prime embarrassment. But I was still happy. After all, I had seen North Korea from as close as anyone could without flying into Pyongyang. And I'd even stepped onto its territory, albeit from the safety of a blue hut in the middle of the Demilitarized Zone.

But now it was time for Mongolia, a country that had intrigued me for years. I remember sitting in a pub telling a friend that one day I would visit Mongolia. He didn't believe me, and deep down, I never thought it would happen either. Yet here I was, with a ticket to Ulaanbaatar on Mongolian Airlines. I finished my second bottle of Cass and went to bed.

Clockwise from top left: One of the many lookout towers that follow the border area with North Korea; A monument at the War Memorial of Korea; A North Korean guard; Two South Korean guards facing North Korea – note the clenched fists; The tense Conference Room, where representatives from both sides occasionally meet; Me standing in North Korea; A rusting train that had lain in the Demilitarized Zone for 56 years

Chapter 13: Genghis Khan and the Mongolian Chokers

No one else I knew had been to Mongolia. Furthermore, I had never come across anyone with an inclination to visit the eighteenth-biggest country in the world. But that wasn't surprising. Mongolia gets the same number of visitors as the Democratic Republic of the Congo, which, unsurprisingly, isn't a lot. Therefore, I was vaguely surprised when I wandered to a distant gate inside Seoul Incheon's vast international airport and discovered that every seat was taken. Most of my fellow passengers looked Chinese, except they were not; they were Mongolians: their possession of more prominent cheekbones, a typical characteristic, was a giveaway. Later, I found out that South Korea boasts the highest number of Mongolians living outside of Mongolia. Many of them work in heavy industry or inside restaurants. The people sitting at the gate were most probably flying home to visit family and friends.

The flight was called and we all shuffled down the air bridge to board the Boeing 767, belonging to MIAT, national airline of Mongolia. It was 2pm and, outside, the day was crisp but chilly. Ulaanbaatar promised to be even colder. Due to its elevation and location, it is the world's coldest capital city, where winter temperatures average minus forty degrees Celsius. Inside the clean cabin, it was nice and warm, and courteous cabin crew directed us to our seats. Five minutes before the posted departure time, the aircraft pushed back from the gate. It was time to go to the land of Genghis Khan.

2

Three hours later, the endless expanse of arid brown lowlands, devoid of all human settlement, was finally giving way to a rising landscape of white. It was as if someone had draped a humungous white cloth over series of hills and then pulled it so the fabric only covered one side. A few minutes later, everything was pure white, broken only by crags and angular mountain tops poking above the ice and snow. Finally, we began our descent into Ulaanbaatar.

Mongolia's capital lies 4430-feet above sea level, nestled in a river valley between mountain ridges and thick coniferous forest that contained wolves, bears and the excellently named Asiatic wild ass. I looked outside as the city came into view. Small houses busy with chimneys, often with traditional yurts (or *gers* are they are usually called in Mongolia) beside them, made up most of the outskirts. When more of Ulaanbaatar appeared, it contained a panorama of smoke belching factories and power stations. What the Mongol hordes would think of their city now, I could only speculate.

We touched down at Genghis Khan International (spelled traditionally as Chinggis Khaan) at 5pm local time. It looked freezing and desolate outside. As we trundled to the terminal, one member of the cabin crew told us the outside temperature was minus two degrees Celsius. At least that was better than the previous week's minus seventeen.

Five minutes later, I was standing in the aisle with my hand luggage. The doors were open and already I could feel an icy chill bearing down upon my neck. I was glad I'd had the forethought to bring my thick coat and hat aboard with me. Both were now donned.

The man in front was carrying a box of strawberries as hand luggage. Another man was grabbing a motorcycle helmet from the overhead bin: just a helmet and nothing else. A woman was carrying a small rice cooker in both hands. Further back, a man was carrying an electric fan heater. He ought to plug it in right now, I thought. Finally, the ragtag collection of passengers and I were released from the aircraft. I found immigration pleasant and efficient, and was quickly welcomed into Mongolia with hardly any fuss. I grabbed my luggage, changed some US dollars into Mongolian tugrik (most of which featured Chinggis Khaan's portrait on the front) and headed outside.

I observed the cows. Three of their kind was munching on some grass at the edge of the airport car park. None were tethered, I noticed, because, as I waited for a taxi, one plodded between some parked cars and laid a cow pat. Then it flicked its tail and walked to a tastier patch of green. Beyond the car park was brown and frosty ground and then, further back, snow-streaked hills.

An old man with a stooped back approached. He offered a one-tooth smile and then produced some postcards from within his thick shawl. I shook my head, looking at the white and green taxi approaching, willing it to speed up. The old geezer flashed the cards in my face. One postcard showed a rosy-cheeked woman standing outside a ger, another depicted a boy milking a goat and the rest were of various buildings that might have been temples.

I jumped in a taxi and left him standing there, open-mouthed and despondent. Feeling sorry for the man, I passed him a 1000-tugrik note (about 30p) through the window. He smiled and walked away.

Another cow loitered by a roundabout, possibly ruminating about whether to eat some grass or to stand about looking stupid. It opted for the latter. Then we passed it, heading away from the airport. Very quickly, Ulaanbaatar came into view: a dirty-brown collection of tower blocks and jutting chimneys, half-finished buildings and skeletal cranes. Without the backdrop of gorgeous mountains, Ulaanbaatar would surely be one of the ugliest cities in Asia.

We passed over a frozen river. Leafless, bare trees stood over the ice, as if wondering when summer would arrive. Up ahead was a huge power station gushing out plumes of white smoke from its dirty chimneys. From the power station's central core, a maze of pipes sprouted hither and thither. One horizontal pipe had steam gushing out, making me think that it was transporting hot water, which it probably was.

The driver hadn't said anything since we set off. He looked vaguely sinister, with thin lips and a shiny head. He was a Bond villain in the making. "Is that a coal power station?" I asked, more to break the silence than to find out the answer. I was pointing to the cooling towers and pipes.

The man looked outside. "No. Hot."

I was nonplussed. "So it's not coal power?"

"Not cold, hot. The Russian people build it." He had clearly misheard my original query, confusing *coal* for *cold*. Soon after, we caught up with the tail end of Ulaanbaatar's notorious traffic. With nothing else to do, I watched a pair of pedestrians walk past. Both were wrapped in thick coats, hats and gloves, their faces angled down to protect against the Tundra-like wind. They were traipsing towards a drab tower block that looked like it belonged to a rough estate in Glasgow, or else in the former Soviet Union. In fact, due to the proliferation of Cyrillic lettering, I could have been in Eastern Europe.

How Mongolia came to have Cyrillic as their official alphabet is interesting. Prior to the 1940s, the official written language was Mongolian, which included characters that resembled Japanese. When hardline communists (Mongolia became a Soviet satellite state in 1924 after Moscow aided their independence from China) pointed out that the Mongolian alphabet was too nationalistic, the president scratched his chin and abolished it, replacing it with the much more conformist Latin script. Anyone who failed to change their shop signs, their menus or their letterheads faced jail or deportation. And so, while people painted new logos above their restaurants and newspaper editors rushed around trying to get new typewriters, the communists pointed out that, really, they should have changed the alphabet to Cyrillic, the language of the Kremlin. The president agreed. Only one month after ordering everyone to change to Latin, he decreed that everyone should use Cyrillic.

So what, you may ask? So what if a country uses Cyrillic or Korean or chooses to use Italian as their official language? It might be a little awkward for people initially, but after that, it should not make any difference to anyone. The problem was that Mongolia (the nation) and Inner Mongolia (a huge part of neighbouring China and home to 25 million people) spoke the same language. Almost overnight, their spoken language remained identical but their written language changed to be something utterly different. They could speak to one another but if one of them tried to write down the conversation, the other would not be able to read it. Imagine an Englishman flying to Australia. When he lands, he can understand any Australian who chooses to speak to him, and he can listen with total comprehension to news reports and TV soap operas. He could go into McDonald's and order a Big Mac and fries without any problem. But – and this is a big but – he would probably find it impossible to read an Australian newspaper, or follow some instructions on the side of an abseiling kit, or to understand the menu at KFC. And this is how it was for Mongolians visiting their neighbours across the border. All because of the strange whims of Mongolian communists in the 1940s. How utterly ridiculous.

4

The UK Foreign Office website states, '*The incidence of violent crime in Ulaanbaatar appears to be on the rise. There has been an increase in reports of foreigners being robbed and assaulted, especially when walking at night.*'

In March 2015, an American national was robbed in a most shocking manner just outside his Ulaanbaatar hotel. Three men came at him from behind and while one choked him, the others robbed him of his belongings. Two days later, another tourist was choked and robbed outside an establishment called the State Department Store. But it didn't end there. Two weeks after that, a female Australian tourist was walking near the State Department Store when three assailants attacked her, again using the choke and rob method. A few days later, a group of men robbed a Swiss man, who was choked and robbed behind the State Department Store. All of which raised the questions: why weren't the police doing something about these chokers and where the hell was this choking hotbed known as the State Department Store?

As well as robbers, tourists in Ulaanbaatar had to be wary of the traffic. It was a well-known fact that every motorist earned a stripe if they hit a pedestrian, two if they got him on a zebra crossing, and three if they knocked him down a manhole. Missing manhole covers were another common problem in the city, with people falling into manholes every day, some dying at the bottom. So chokers, traffic and manholes were on my list of things to avoid, it seemed.

We passed a line of modern buildings, probably apartments for the elite of Ulaanbaatar. At their bases were a series of hairdressers, pizzerias and banks, plus a few karaoke bars. Then we passed a tank. It was perched on an angular plinth in front of a newly constructed shiny glass building that might have been a shopping mall or a corporate headquarters. "Good tank," I said to the driver, hoping he would slow down so I could get a better look.

He nodded and gunned the accelerator. "It is Russian."

I wondered whether everything in Mongolia was Russian, but didn't have time to consider this because we were bumping over a railway line flanked with electricity pylons and dreary apartment blocks. These ones were not for the elite, I hazarded. They looked grim, dirty and crime-ridden. One presented a large advertisement for a snooker hall. The poster featured a close-up photo of former snooker world champion, Stephen Hendry. Unfortunately, the name of the establishment was the Hendy Snooker Club.

And then we arrived at my hotel. I gave the driver a wad of tugrik, grabbed my bags and rushed inside before a choker could get me in their sights.

5

The Kempinski Khan Palace, my hotel, was on the corner of Peace Avenue, a more-or-less straight road that ran east to west, cutting through the entire length of the city. My room looked out across its honking intersection, thick with cars and buses. A policeman stood in their midst, blowing his whistle and pointing as if he was in charge, which he was. Behind the junction were more god-awful apartment blocks, a fixture of downtown Ulaanbaatar, as well as something called the Somang Plaza, a shiny glass covered shopping mall that boasted *Good Price!* on its side. Further back were the glorious snow-topped ranges that led to the Bogd Khan Mountain, a 3000ft monster that looked down upon Southern Ulaanbaatar.

Before it got too dark and the chokers came out to play, I wanted to venture outside to find a grocery store. I put on two jumpers, a thick coat, my woolly hat and some thermal gloves. I put my passport, phone and laptop inside the safe and, after removing a little bit of cash, checked the mirror. If a choking gang were in operation, they would get scant offerings from me. Mind you, I looked like a mugger myself, especially with my gloves and burglar hat.

Evening was settling in over the cold streets of Ulaanbaatar. Instead of heading down to the busy junction, I turned uphill, along a road called Ikh Toiruu. A long line of commercial blocks was across from me, each more ugly than the last. I spied a plastic sign attached to the column of a street light. It advertised a place with the fascinating name of *Hennessy's X,O CLUB*, the placement of the comma unexpectedly intriguing. It was close to the *Seattle Rest and Pub*, a brick establishment that reeked of a 1970s council estate. Next door was a billiard hall where a group of young men had chosen to loiter, drinking cans of beer and smoking cigarettes. They looked like potential chokers; I quickened my pace. None paid me any attention as I passed.

Finally, I came to a supermarket, or СУПЕРМАРКЕТ, as it was written. I climbed some steps, bypassed a swaying drunkard and entered. Its shelves were full of dumplings, noodles, husks of bread plus bottles of beer and vodka. At the rear was a meat section that was closed, but a dairy portion that was still open. I considered buying some yak cheese and milk to go with some dumplings but walked instead to a large section dedicated to candy, pausing at the gaudy colours until I spotted what I was looking for: a fridge. Once there, I picked out a couple of bottles of Altan Gobi, the local beer, and some strange meat that might have been ham or chicken to go with the bread rolls I'd already picked up. When I placed it all on the counter, the harridan behind the till barked something at me, presumably the price.

"English?" I asked, more hopeful than expectant.

The woman looked up with scorn in her eyes. *Actual scorn.* It was as if I'd asked where I could find a place to eat live hamsters in front of their owners. She said something else and looked at her watch. I offered her a wad of tugrik, but the woman shook her head. I offered more, but she shook her head again and tutted. I didn't know what else to do, which made her grab a 5000-tugrik note (£2.20) from my hand. Tutting again, she unlocked her till and counted out my change, all the while shaking her head and making it plainly clear she wanted to choke me to death. I thanked her in Russian, which brought another scowl of irritation.

I exited the shop with my booty, retracing my steps to the hotel. It was freezing and snow falling. From the heat of tropical Africa to the frozen hinterlands of Mongolia in the space of a week: my body was in confusion. I escaped the winter chill and entered the plush lobby of the Kempinski. With my meal fit for a king in my shopping bag, I retired to my room. The next day I would see the sights of Ulaanbaatar.

6

The next afternoon was crisp and sunny. Temperatures were hovering around zero, but the sky was a stunning blue. Ulaanbaatar's infamous pollution (due to coal-burning power stations and the sheer amount of wood burnt in people's homes for heating) would not be bothering me today. I walked down the hill to the intersection. The zebra crossing lines were faded, and impatient vehicles covered what wasn't. With the little green man flashing, I ran across, reaching the safety of the other side with barely a second to spare.

I made my way along Peace Avenue, passing the Somang Plaza, still proudly boasting itself as a Good Price market. The British Embassy in Mongolia was on my right – a large white, well groomed building set back from the potholes, ice and traffic. Pleasingly, its entrance was unguarded and unfenced and, if I had chosen to, I could have walked up the door and gone in. Near it was a contender for Worst Looking Piece of Architecture in Ulaanbaatar – the hideous XacBank building. It was a cube of ugly concrete, rendered in dirty beige and then streaked with white clumps of flaking paint. And yet, despite the ugly buildings, the cracked pavements, the beeping traffic, the cold and the possibility of being mugged, I was enjoying myself. I was in a brand new country, wandering along a street in a city I had once only dreamed of visiting. I pulled my hat tighter and smiled a secret smile.

I came to the Wrestling Palace, a large red and white, circular building with a flying saucer-shaped roof. Wrestling is big business in Mongolia, where competitions can last for days. Brass bands knock out jaunty tunes while large, bare-chested men grapple and try to get each other to the ground. Unfortunately, the palace was closed for winter.

Further into my Peace Avenue amble, I traversed a bridge that spanned a dirty, semi-frozen river. Slushy brown water meandered around tufts of overgrown grass. Halfway across was a series of small street stalls. At one sat a red-cheeked woman on a collapsible chair. Her little stall sold cigarettes, folds of sheepskin, chocolate bars, lollies on sticks and packs of chewing gum. With my mouth so dry, I stopped to buy a packet of the gum, and the woman smiled a grin so broad that it reached all the way across the wide expanse of her face.

"Spasibah!" she said thanking me, clearly thinking I was Russian.

"Spasibah," I replied, causing her to smile even more. This woman should get a job in the supermarket near my hotel, I thought.

About half an hour after leaving my hotel, I arrived at my first destination: Chinggis Khaan Square, the heart of Ulaanbaatar.

7

The square was huge, but to get to it I had to walk through a patch of greenery called the Chinggis Khaan Park. Someone had shovelled mounds of snow away from the paths and onto the frozen grass. Patches of ice still lurked unseen, waiting to catch out unsuspecting pedestrians. I nimbly avoided the patches and found myself at the southern end of the square. At the northern end, some way into the distance, was the imposing Parliament Building, a wide expanse of white columns, sweeping marble steps and sheets of blue glass. I walked towards it, passing a grand statue of a warrior sitting on a horse. His name was Damdin Sukhbaatar, a nineteenth century revolutionary hero who featured heavily on lower denomination Mongolian banknotes. Beyond him, at the entrance to the Parliament Building, was another gigantic statue, this one of the great man himself, Chinggis Khaan, seated and resting his arms on the edge of his oversized throne. The legendary founder of the great Mongol Empire resembled Buddha.

Standing close to him was a soldier. He was wearing camouflaged fatigues that sported a thick furry collar. An equally thick and furry hat covered his head. He had thrust his hands deep into layered pockets, watching five elderly men walking down the steps of the parliament. They shuffled carefully and slowly, balancing on each other from time to time, mindful of the ice. All five were wearing *deels*, colourful traditional clothing resembling tunics, each a different colour: olive green, sky blue, orange, red and brown. Though deels were common attire for nomadic herders outside of the cities, it was only the elderly who commonly wore such clothing in Ulaanbaatar,

A car zipped by driven by a toddler. A few more electric-powered plastic vehicles zigzagged around in the space between the statue and the Parliament building. A woman sat nearby, waiting with more vehicles for hire. The five old men eventually made it to the bottom of the steps and found a bench to chew the fat and smoke cigarettes. They were clearly friends, happy in each other's company. I left them to it and wandered to the western edge of the square. A huge white building that might have been a palace, but was probably a bank, lay at right angles to the Parliament. The Mongolian Stock Exchange was just along from it and, on the eastern side, was the Opera House and National Art Gallery. Chinggis Square was most definitely the place to be in Ulaanbaatar. But for me, it was time to move on.

8

Walking further along Peace Avenue, something made me pause for thought. It was not the traffic snarling around me and nor was it the slippery, frost-coated pavement beneath my feet. No, it was something far more sinister: the hotbed of chokers, no less. I had inadvertently stumbled across the State Department Store. I gulped and walked past it, pressing my chin close to my chest to thwart any would-be assailants.

Nothing happened.

I stopped and walked back across its front façade. People were going in; others were coming out. A group of teenage girls sauntered past me, and not one of them tried to choke me into submission. Emboldened by this, I decided to enter Mongolia's largest shopping mall, a leftover piece of architecture from the nation's Soviet era.

I found an escalator and plenty of shops, including one that offered *Italian Elegance Shoes*. I discovered that, instead of employing people with large hands, the State Department Store employed helpful people who wanted to assist me across all of its seven floors. On the top floor was a department store with large windows. I walked past some ornaments and looked out. The view of central Ulaanbaatar was not pretty by any stretch of the imagination, but it had a certain charm. The mountains helped, and so did the snow-streaked roofs. To celebrate my bravery at entering *Choker Central,* I almost bought a stuffed yak, but common sense prevailed, and I exited the State Department Store onto the street.

I passed the homely-sounding *British Shop.* From the outside, it looked how a Polish Shop might look in a British town: run down and sad. A couple of faded Union Jack graphics flanked the name of the shop. I went inside, hoping to hear the tinkling of a bell, but all I got was a creaking door. Inside was smaller than I expected and, instead of Polish sausages and Zywiec lager, much of its stock was either foodstuff from Asda and Tesco, or else tourist items such as London snow globes, small plastic flags and Tower of London keyrings. Was there a market for such things in Ulaanbaatar, I wondered? Did people really need to buy Asda's own brand gravy in Mongolia? Clearly they did, because one shelf was full of it. I left the shop and headed back to the hotel to warm up.

9

The next day was cold – minus five, in fact. But the sky was cloudless as I wandered back along Peace Avenue in search of a Buddhist monastery that the hotel recommended I should see. "Very nice," the woman in the lobby had said. "You will like much."

On the map, it didn't seem far to walk but with Chinggis Khaan Square a long way behind me, and my feet beginning to hurt, I realised I should have caught a taxi. After another eternity of plodding along, I finally turned uphill, leaving the busy traffic behind me. The new road looked decrepit, home to stray dogs (mostly lounging around asleep, thankfully), dingy bars and former Communist-era apartment blocks that needed to be condemned. Some distance along, the brick buildings thinned and a shantytown replaced them. A broken wooden fence surrounded a collection of roughly-built stone shacks and dingy gers. Whether the fence was to stop people getting in or to thwart residents from leaving, I couldn't tell.

The outskirts of the city were reportedly worse. Ger districts – areas without access to running water and power – were growing alarmingly quickly around Ulaanbaatar. In fact, over a third of the city's population lived in these areas of high poverty. Burning coal and powering wood stoves was the only way they could keep themselves warm. This added massively to the city's pollution problem.

I hiked up the incline, passing more sleeping dogs, wondering how they could slumber in such cold temperatures until finally, after almost an hour's walking, I arrived at the Gandantegchinlen Monastery complex, Ulaanbaatar's most popular tourist site. Unsurprisingly, I was the only visitor there.

Compared to the Buddhist temples I'd seen in Seoul, the monastery was nothing special. Still, it was reportedly home to a few hundred saffron-robed monks, and so I expected it to be a place of tranquillity, but it was more like an oversized car park, at least along its outer walls. Parked vehicles, prowling taxis and darting and cooing pigeons awaited me. The pigeons were gathered around a stone temple because someone had scattered hundreds of seeds there. I saw a monk jump into a taxi, which surprised me. For some reason, I expected Buddhist monks to walk everywhere. Pondering this oddity, I entered the complex not expecting to be impressed.

Yet I was.

The main temple, though not as large or as colourful as any I'd seen in Seoul, was still striking. It was a stout white block of stone, topped with a multi-tiered green roof, and finished with an abundance of golden decorations. I walked up to its entrance, heading towards a prayer wheel in its courtyard. A young woman in front of me was ringing small bells that hung from its ornamental centre. Incense smoke wafted outwards as she walked clockwise around it. I passed her and entered the monastery.

It was cramped, but that was because a gigantic golden statue of Avalokiteśvara (a Buddhist lord who looks down upon the Earth) took up most of the room. The figure stretched from the floor to the ceiling, and later I found out it was one of the tallest indoor statues in the world. The woman who had been by the prayer wheel came in and began to pray at the front. Not wanting to intrude, I walked around a side section of the massive statue, noticing hundreds of Buddhas, each one small and golden, sitting inside its own personal glass case. All of them were lucky to have survived the great religious purge of the 1930s, when the vast majority of Ulaanbaatar's monasteries were demolished or handed over to communists. The only one they kept was the one in which I was now standing.

10

After lunch, I got the hotel to ring a taxi for me. I wanted to see one more thing before my time in Ulaanbaatar came to an end, but couldn't face the hour-and-a-half walk to get there.

The driver was a man called Bayar, in his late twenties, who could speak English. As we set off to see the Zaisan Memorial in the south of the city, he told me that he was a new father. He was clearly excited about this, as well he should be. "She is only two months old and is the centre of my life."

I asked what his daughter's name was.

"Altantsetseg. It means 'golden flower'."

Threading past depressing apartment blocks as we slowly made our way towards the mountains, Bayar pressed on the radio. It was a news bulletin in Mongolian, which he listened to for about three seconds before switching it off. He pressed the CD play button instead. Wizzard's 1970s hit *I Wish it Could be Christmas Every Day* began sounding through the car's tinny speakers. It seemed a strange choice, and later, when Wham's *Last Christmas* started playing, I concluded that Bayar was a fan of UK festive hits. When the song was almost over, he asked me what I thought of Ulaanbaatar. I told him it was a bit grubby in places, and the traffic was bad, but I liked it nonetheless. That was the truth. The Mongolian capital was one of those increasingly rare cities that was still genuine. It was not catering to holidaymakers (it was too far off any traditional tourist trails for that) and was not trying to show off to anyone. Ulaanbaatar was what it was: rough, ready and real.

"The traffic is getting worse every year," Bayar offered. In front of us was a snake of cars. Ahead of them was a line of mountains. Without the concrete, I could've been in the Alps. "I used to drive across the city in twenty minutes. Not now; it takes two hours."

This particular journey took almost half an hour, but, before we got to the Zaisan Memorial, we stopped at the tank I'd seen on the way in from the airport. Both of us climbed out to see it up close and, when I couldn't decipher the information etched onto its placard, Bayar stepped in as interpreter.

"The tank was part of a Soviet brigade," he said.

I waited for him to say more, because there was more writing than just that, but when Bayar didn't offer anything further, I walked to the other side of the large plinth to look at a map. This I could decipher myself because it only had two words: Moscow and Berlin. Between these two cities was the route the tank had taken to fight the Germans. How it ended up in Ulaanbaatar was a mystery that even stumped Bayar. We headed back to the car.

11

As Paul McCartney sang about a *Wonderful Christmas Time*, Bayar asked whether the music was okay. I paused answering, not wanting to offend. When I didn't say anything, Bayar said, "Because it is the only English CD I have. Someone left it in my taxi. If you don't like it, I'll switch it off."

"No, it's fine."

He nodded and left the festive tune to waft through the car. "So are you ready for the climb?"

"I thought we were driving?"

"We are, but there are still many steps to climb: six hundred from the bottom, three hundred from the car park."

While I fretted over this unexpected news, we pulled up into a small car park full of vehicles. Even though it was freezing cold, with spots of sleet fluttering around, people were out in force to see the old Soviet monument, built in honour of soldiers killed in the Second World War. We stepped out to join them.

Soviet influence in Mongolia began in the 1920s and didn't really end until the collapse of the Soviet Union in 1989. The Zaisian Memorial was just one of the reminders of that period. We began the trek upward; by the half-way stage, I was on the verge of collapse. Pretending to take a photo of the panoramic view of Ulaanbaatar that sprawled before me, I waited for my heart rate to slow, which I could actually hear pounding through my ears, which I didn't think was a good sign. But the view was incredible, covering most of the city. I could see the tower blocks and billowing chimneys. I gazed over rough ground that only yaks might graze upon and my eyes spied construction sites for tomorrow's shiny new skyscrapers. From my perch, the city looked glorious.

Bayar waited patiently for me to take some photos. When I'd recovered the power of speech, I commented on his fitness levels.

"I am a kick boxer," he told me. "I have to work out a lot. I was in Beijing a few months ago for a competition where I won three medals."

"Wow! You must be good?"

He looked bashful. "I am a *master*."

We carried on to the top, each step harder than the last, but it was worth it in the end. The memorial dripped with pure *Soviet* delight, and I loved it. The central core was a circular concrete display with colourful murals on the inside. The artwork presented the Soviets as the valiant warriors, quashing the Japanese and Nazis into submission while cuddling Mongolian children. But the most striking thing about the memorial was the massive brave-faced Soviet soldier. His gallant concrete face looked down across Ulaanbaatar.

Feeling the chill of winter, I moved to a position where part of the memorial offered respite against the wind. Behind me was a crop of hills and high land. In their shadows sat the new developments of Ulaanbaatar: luxury apartment blocks, shopping malls and cinemas. Bayar told me that only rich people could afford to live there. "Rent expensive, maybe two million tugrik per week." That equated to around £700/month, which was well in excess of the average city wage of 800,000 tugrik/month (£300). "But they will be near that American school. That is the best school in Ulaanbaatar. You can see it down there."

I looked. The American School was a modern, blue-roofed building set in the midst of the new developments. Some of its classrooms would look upon a majestic Alpine scene. But for me, it was time to head back to the city. The snow was really starting to come down, and the last thing I needed was to be stranded outside the city. Back at the Kempinski, I thanked Bayar for his time and his expertise as an impromptu guide, paying him a healthy tip. Mongolia was almost done and China beckoned on the southern horizon.

Clockwise from top left: Chinggis Khaan on the lower tugrik banknote; The Zaisan Memorial, an old Soviet memorial; Old men wearing deels (traditional dress) chewing the fat in Chinggis Khaan Square; Gandantegchinlen Monastery complex, Ulaanbaatar's most popular tourist site; A Mongolian solider keeping the peace in Ulaanbaatar: The State Department Store – hotbed of chokers

Chapter 14: Beijing, Beijing, Beijing

Beijing hadn't originally been part of my mammoth Africa to Asia itinerary. What changed this was when I found out about China's tourist-friendly 72-hour visa-free travel arrangement. All I had to do was land in China, and then leave by the same airport before the 72 hours were up, and I wouldn't need a costly visa, entailing ridiculous form filling and moments of stress.

But my trip to Beijing didn't start in a friendly manner.

"No! No!" snapped the woman standing in the aisle of the Air China Boeing 737. We had just reached cruise altitude en route to Beijing and she had caught me red-handed committing a most heinous act aboard a commercial aircraft: listening to music. After removing my earphones, I tried smiling at the burgundy-uniformed woman. She didn't smile back; instead, she shook her finger. "No allowed! No music, no phone. Nothing! Switch off now! Or I kill you!"

She didn't say this last bit, but she thought it – I could tell. Rolling my eyes turned out to be a mistake.

"I no want trouble from you, sir," the woman hissed. "Turn off phone, now!"

I nodded and showed the woman that my phone was in airplane mode.

The woman shook her head in rapid succession. "No airplane, no flight mode – just off! Off!"

She actually waited for me to turn off the power and then demanded to see the black screen. Finally, she nodded and walked away, leaving me with three hours to fill by staring around the inside of a passenger jet. I couldn't even look outside because I was in an aisle seat. With no book to keep me entertained, I watched the comedy show on the screen dangling from the panel ahead of me. It was one of these shows where unsuspecting members of the public are faced with unusual situations created by teams of actors. Every airline in the world had bought into these programs. I hated them.

We landed at Beijing Capital International Airport at just after 2.30pm, where I fought my way through the crowds in order to find immigration. Lines were everywhere, with hundreds, if not thousands, of people standing in them. I scanned the front of the first few lines for information. Most said *Foreigner*. I wondered whether to join one to accept the long wait, but decided to walk along the huge immigration room in search of a shorter queue. The problem with this, though, was that everybody else was doing the same thing and, if I didn't make my move soon, then I'd be waiting even longer.

Then I saw salvation: a queue with no one in it. The electronic display above it read: 72-hour visa. I skipped to the desk and was processed in less than two minutes. Hail China and its 72-hour visa rule. It made up for the three-and-a-half hour flight of misery.

2

Beijing was basking in sunshine. The expected and infamous fog was nowhere in sight. The traffic was bad, though, far worse than even Ulaanbaatar's. Gridlock snaked in both directions on a highway flanked by tall, modern skyscrapers. If not for the Chinese lettering on them, I might have been anywhere in Miami. My taxi lurched forward, charging into the lane to our right. Someone beeped. So did someone else. Another space appeared to my left and a bus nipped in. More angry beeps.

"Google banned," said the taxi driver, a thin, middle-aged man with only a few wisps of hair left on his crown. He didn't seem bothered by the traffic.

"I beg your pardon?"

"Google banned. Same Facebook."

It seemed an unusual thing to say, and I wondered what had brought about the comment, but before I had chance to ponder, we swung off the highway, making a death-defying turn along an underpass before emerging onto a quieter road.

"Two million people, their job in China is check other people not using Google," the driver added, almost cryptically.

While I worked out what he meant, we pulled up outside the Inner Mongolia Grand Hotel Wangfujing, a hefty title for a hefty hotel. I said, "So you're saying that two million people in China have jobs which entail them checking up that the rest of the population are not using Google?"

"That what I say. But I get special phone for you, yeh? Google is okay. Facebook is okay. You wan buy?"

I declined and climbed out of the taxi, mentally commending the man on his entrepreneurial spirit. Later I found out he was correct, though. Google and Facebook were banned in China, and so were Twitter, Instagram and YouTube. The Great Firewall of China was long and far reaching.

The Inner Mongolia Grand Hotel featured a lobby dripping with marble. A man with a big brush was polishing the floor while another man ran a cloth over a pair of huge ornamental horses. After dropping my things in the room, I was back in the lobby, asking a courteous man about the best way to get to Tiananmen Square. He told me it would take about thirty minutes to walk or I could, he suggested, catch a metro train. "Very easy. No problem for you. Go to Dongdan Station – just along from here – and then a few stops to Tiananmen West metro stop. But you have to hurry; square closes for visitors at 5pm."

That left just over an hour. I thanked him and, armed with only my camera and some money, I set forth for prime Chinese adventure.

3

I found Dondgan Station easily enough. That was the easy part of the adventure ticked off. Buying a ticket proved easy too, because the machine offered English that even a simpleton could read. Armed with it, I headed to the crowded platform, busy with people heading home after a day in Beijing. I had timed my journey badly, I realised: the rush hour was almost upon us, but there was nothing I could do about that now. If I didn't see Tiananmen Square tonight, then I wouldn't have any other time, so when the silver train with the red stripe along its length pulled up, and the crowd pushed me aboard, I accepted my fate. Adventures were sometimes not easy.

I could not recall a single time when I'd been aboard a fuller train. But at least the crush meant I did not have to hold onto the handrails or dangling hoops. Like a milk bottle in a crate, I simply went with the flow. Except the flow was in the wrong direction.

I realised this after three stops. None of the stops I needed had come up, meaning I had boarded the wrong train. Waiting to alight at the next stop, a middle-aged man a few feet away raised his phone, angled it towards me and then took my photo. I knew he had taken my photo because I could see the resulting image on his screen. Satisfied with his not-so-sneaky-shot, he put his camera away and looked at his shoes.

I was astounded. Firstly, at how brazen he was, and secondly, why he wanted to take my photo in the first place. It was an invasion of my privacy! I looked around to see if anyone else had noticed his antics, but everyone was either engrossed in their own phone or reading a newspaper. When the train hissed to a stop, I glared at the man. He smiled back. I left the train and then, ten minutes later, resumed my journey in the opposite direction.

At Tiananmen West metro stop, I followed a convoluted subterranean route that delivered me to a metal detector. While I waited in the line for a security guard to check I wasn't carrying bombs, a platoon of green-uniformed soldiers marched past, each in perfect step. All looked young, barely in their adulthood, yet all looked ready for battle.

My belongings passed muster and I climbed some stone steps into natural light. I was on a main stretch of road that epitomised *old* China. Gone were the skyscrapers and advertising boards, replaced by ornamental gardens, colourful pagodas with multi-layered, curled-up roof sections. This was more like it, I thought to myself. And then, after a brief walk along the road, I came to the square itself.

4

Everybody of a certain age remembers Tiananmen Square for one thing: Tank Man. Images and footage of the incident involving Tank Man flashed across the world's TV screens in 1989. They showed a young man wearing smart black trousers and a white shirt standing in front of a column of tanks. He was carrying a shopping bag in each hand. As the lead tank rumbles toward Tank Man, he doesn't move out of the way. Seemingly at a loss as to what else to do, the tank stops. The tanks behind are forced to stop too. By going forward, they will crush the man; by staying put, they are accepting defeat.

The man, whose identity has never been disclosed, was playing a dangerous game. In the days prior to his stand, the army had killed scores of people in Beijing, most of them students protesting against Chinese rule. Standing in front of a tank seemed apparent suicide. In the end, though, the tank commander did what any sane person would do: he went around the man. Meanwhile, hidden from view in hotels up the street, Western news crews were filming it all.

Tank Man watched the tank move over and, for a few moments, it looked like he was going to accept this, but then he ran in front of the tank once more. Man and Tank repeated the dance a few seconds later. Then, to break the deadlock, Tank Man climbed onto the stationary tank and started shouting through gaps in the armour. Then he climbed onto the turret and yelled down the hatch. After this, he jumped off and stood in front of the tank again. Finally, two men approach Tank Man and pull him away.

No one knows what happened to the silent protestor after this. Or, if they do, they are not saying. There are some claims that the Chinese government executed him, others say he is living as a farmer in the countryside. I recall watching the footage at the time, thinking how brave that man was. He would have been around my age then, and the closest thing to a protest I'd been involved in was not tidying my bedroom. If Tank Man is still alive, he will be in his mid-forties.

5

Tiananmen Square was massive: one of the largest squares in the world, in fact. Stately buildings surrounded all four sides, with monuments, flags and eagle-eyed sentries dotted around the centre. At one end of the square is Tiananmen Gate, which featured a huge portrait of Chairman Mao. Beyond the gate was the Forbidden City, something I would be visiting the next day.

I gazed up at the portrait of the most famous Chinaman in history. His image was pleasingly clean and free of pollution or traffic fume stains. Mao's stately likeness made him look friendly and wise: a distinguished leader. During the student protests of 1989, someone threw eggs at the portrait. When officials apprehended the perpetrator, they sentenced him to life imprisonment. In 2010, when someone threw a bottle of ink towards the portrait, but missed, guards wrestled him to the ground. His fate is unknown.

I entered the square, aware of all the security cameras homing in on me. Policemen were everywhere (both uniformed and plain clothed), as were fire extinguishers. The latter were in case anyone tried to set themselves on fire. In 2001, five people entered Tiananmen Square, set themselves alight and killed themselves. More recently, in 2011, a 42-year old Chinese man, unhappy with the outcome of a recent court case, set himself on fire in the square. Only the quick-thinking action of a policeman, who luckily had a fire extinguisher on his motorbike, saved him. Since then, fire extinguishers are a common sight across the square.

No one looked like they were about to set themselves on fire, so I walked around the edge of the square, taking in the National

Museum of China, the Great Hall of the People (a building so long that it covered the same length as five Boeing 747s), and the Chairman Mao Memorial Building, which sat within the square, guarded by straight-faced sentries at all corners. Inside was the embalmed body of the great man himself, encased inside a crystal coffin. Unfortunately, it was closed.

A man rushed over to me. He was a geeky Chinese man wearing thick-rimmed black glasses. At first, I thought he might be a secret policeman coming to tell me off, but I quickly ascertained that he wanted to take my photo. His wife was behind him, and when I nodded, he passed his camera to her and stood awkwardly next to me, grinning like a loon. She pressed the button and then took another for good luck.

What was it with Chinese (and Korean schoolgirls) when it came to Westerners? Never in a million years would I go up to a Chinese man in London and ask for a photo. And neither would I try to sneak one of him on a busy tube train. It was only later that I learned that the vast majority of Chinese people have never seen a foreign face with their own eyes. The man on the train, and the couple in Tiananmen Square, were most probably Chinese nationals who lived in the countryside and therefore were tourists themselves. When they saw a Western face, it was a novel experience for them, and the only way to remember it was to take a photo.

With the cold biting my skin and with 5pm approaching quickly, I had one last, lingering look across Tiananmen Square. I nodded my head in appreciation and left.

6

Fried bullfrog, hot blood soup and the scrumptious-sounding braised sheep entrails were on offer inside the menu from Hell. I scanned down more of the list, discounting fried pig's ear and mashed sheep skull (whole), pondering whether to go for one of the simpler choices on offer, which included intestine, brain or tongue. Crispy black fungus sounded like the safest best, but then I turned the page and saw a photo of something that looked even nicer. It showed a set of meaty things, temptingly sliced and nestled on a bed of lettuce, with some tomatoes adding a splash of colour. They were sliced pig's feet cooked by Beelzebub himself.

In the end, I opted for chicken gizzards with roasted horse testicles. Except they didn't have it on the menu. Instead, I ordered something called beef in sauce. The young waitress seemed amused that I'd actually made an order. As she wrote my choice on her little notepad, she could barely suppress a giggle.

"Yu won ho?" she asked.

I let the request reverberate around my brain for a second. Was she asking whether I wanted a whore? It seemed unlikely but not entirely out of the question considering the surreal nature of the menu. I looked up quizzically.

"Ho' or cole?"

"Hot," I answered. As if I'd want a cold meal of beef and sauce. I was not on a camping trip in the Himalayas.

"Ho?" she seemed surprised.

"Yes please. Piping hot, and a beer too."

She nodded, giggled and wrote something else down. Off she trotted.

For my enjoyment, the restaurant featured a small stage. Suddenly, without warning, a man carrying a drum walked onto it and sat down. I turned to watch him, as did a few other patrons of the restaurant. The drummer was wearing traditional clothing, and was soon joined by another man. The newcomer had a stringed instrument about his person. And then some women joined them, and soon all four were cavorting to a tune that was instantly grating. When the dance ended, I felt compelled to clap, even though I was the only one to do so.

My beer came, and I drank it thirstily, which turned out to be an error of judgement because when my meal arrived, it was not just hot, it was *fiery*. When the waitress had asked whether I wanted it hot, she meant spicy. The beef in sauce was the hottest thing I'd ever tasted, and the instant a drop of the satanic sauce touched my tongue, it was on fire. My lips burned, blistered and then turned numb in the space of two seconds. I downed the remainder of my Tao Beer and ordered another. As I tried another mouthful of the scorching food, one of the performers produced a microphone and started screeching into it. Then she had a fit, or so it seemed, before bowing demurely at me. I clapped, with tears of pain dripping down my reddened face.

"You like?" asked the waitress, who had suddenly appeared.

I was crying but I nodded and gave a thumbs up: the usual British response. But I couldn't eat another thing, and even the beer was giving me aftershocks. There was only one thing for it: I would retire to my room and eat my *Numb and Spicy Hot Pot* flavour crisps. I only wish I were joking.

7

The next morning I was in the lobby looking for my guide. All I knew was that he was called Jack and he would meet me at 8am. Jack sounded Western, but he probably wasn't. Many Chinese people went by Western names so that foreigners could avoid the embarrassment of saying their Chinese names incorrectly.

A flight crew arrived. I recognised the cabin crew uniforms as Etihad, from the many times I'd flown with them. I watched them walk to the desk, and then had a wander around the horse sculptures. It offered a good vantage point of the doors. A young woman walked in, and then a man in his thirties. Could he be Jack? The man was loitering near the entrance as if looking for someone. I boldly walked up to him and our eyes met. "Hi," I said. "Are you a guide for the Great Wall?"

The man shook his head. "Not guide. Manager of hotel."

"Mr Jason!" said a woman's voice. It was the young woman. "I am guide for you. I am very pleased to meet you." She led me to one side, leaving the manager to manage whatever task he was doing.

Her name was Susan (as she called herself), and she was in her mid-twenties, a former university student, and now a full time guide. I shook her proffered hand. "I was expecting someone called Jack..."

"Ah, yes. Mr Jack work in office. He no come out."

Susan was bubbling with excitement. Whether it was an act, or whether it was genuine, it was infectious and, as she led me out to the car and driver (a sixty-something man who spoke not a word of English), I warmed to her immediately.

"You pilot?" she asked as I buckled my seatbelt.

I told her I wasn't.

"Not a pilot? That surprises me. I thought you would be pilot. All other tourist from your hotel have been pilot. They stay in hotel and do tour with me."

After assuring her I was not a pilot, Susan outlined how the tour would look. First, we would drive to the Forbidden City, then make a stop at a silk factory. Following that, we would drive for about an hour, stop for lunch, and then visit the Great Wall of China. "Is itinerary okay for you, Mr Jason?"

Everything was, apart from the silk factory. I had no wish to visit a shop to get a hard sell for a product I didn't want. I told Susan as much.

"Oh, no, Mr Jason. It will be nothing like that. You will enjoy the visit and you will learn many things. All of my other clients have enjoyed seeing how silk is made."

What could I say? I could refuse and then upset Susan, no doubt jeopardising any chance of her receiving recompense from the shop in question. Or I could just accept things for what they were and enjoy my day, which was precisely what I did.

8

Even though 14 million people a year visit the Forbidden City, I had no real idea of what it actually was. After parking, Susan led me to a long queue that fed towards a fancy metal detector. One queue was for men, the other for women and, once through the other side, we met under the portrait of Chairman Mao, the same one I'd seen the previous evening.

Susan went into guide mode. "So through here is the start of the Forbidden City. Before the revolution, it was the Imperial Palace of the Ming Dynasty, but now it is called the Forbidden City. You may think the name means no one could enter except the royal family, but this is incorrect. The name is because it was forbidden to enter or leave the place without the Emperor's permission."

I nodded, staring through the arches, trying to see something of interest. While Susan prattled on about the layout (rectangular), the individual buildings (almost one thousand) and then started talking about the moat and walls, I tried to stifle a yawn. It was all very interesting hearing facts but all I wanted was to step through an arch so I could see it for myself. Perhaps sensing my impatience, Susan told me to follow her.

The other side was a hotbed of ticket queues, tour groups (all led by flag-waving guides) and snack stalls. Some tall and palace-like buildings lay further back, close enough to entice but too far to savour properly. Susan gave me strict instructions to stay put while she bought the tickets. I nodded and two minutes later grew so bored that I went to look at the snack stalls. Crisps and cans of Coke were on offer, both items selling well due to the number of people passing through. I was about to buy some crisps when two Chinese women accosted me, babbling away and gesturing at their camera.

Here we go again, I thought. I dutifully posed with both women, one after the other, while photos were taken and smiles were shared. When they finished, another woman rushed over. Soon a small queue formed and I felt like a film star. Wondering how to extract myself from the unusual situation, I saw Susan heading my way. She looked amused, but led me to safety. I looked over my shoulder and saw a man filming me.

"They always find the foreigner," Susan said. "But it is unusual for so many of them to want photos. I think a big group has come to Beijing on vacation. The only Westerners they see are on TV."

"Maybe they think I am famous?" I quipped.

"I do not think so."

Charming. Don't mince your words, love.

9

For the next hour, Susan and I wandered from palace to palace, with her giving a running commentary on every building, on every dragon carving and on every monument we came across. She knew the best places to take photos from, and in some of these locations, she made me pose for them. I grinned in front of the Hall of Supreme Harmony and puckered in front of the Palace of Heavenly Purity. I stuck my arms out by an ancient tree with gnarled branches, and I pouted in front of a gilded lion statue.

"Mr Jason," squeaked Susan. "Please smile for the camera. Don't frown."

I forced a lopsided grin as I posed in the Imperial Garden. The resulting image made me look like a deviant. Over the next half an hour, Susan took about a hundred photos of me. I later deleted almost every one of them.

The Forbidden City was impressive, though. The grandeur and size of some of the palace buildings was something to behold. Even the thousands of people could not take away from the sheer wonder of it all. The only problem was that no one was allowed inside any of the palaces, and so we were forced to crowd around windows and doors with mobile phones, video cameras and reaching hands. Luckily, for me, I was taller than most Chinese people were but, even so, I quickly grew weary of fighting to the front in order to take a picture of a fancy throne or a bronze crane statue.

One building we were allowed to enter was the Imperial Telephone Bureau. An old wooden telephone, complete with a rudimentary mouthpiece, sat on a small desk. For some reason, possibly due to the colour and the big bells that looked like eyes, it reminded me of Scooby Doo. Built in the early 1900s, the room was China's first telephone exchange, used in the burgeoning era of science and discovery when even the Emperor saw the importance of communication with the world outside his palace complex. Speaking of the outside world, it was time for Susan and me to depart the Forbidden City and find our driver. We were due to visit the silk factory.

10

The man in the white lab coat looked efficiently scientist-like. His thick black glasses added to the effect, as did his clinically clean fingernails. Since I was a solo tourist, I had his whole spiel to myself, especially since Susan had cited a toilet break to take a leave of absence. Before he went into his silkworm laboratory, the man pointed to four large photographs on the wall. In each of them, the same smiling man, decked out in a fetching crimson-buttoned tunic, was shaking hands with a visiting dignitary. I recognised two of them as the Sultan of Brunei and President George Bush.

"The man in the tunic," said Mr Scientist, "is our proud owner. The others are important visitors to factory. Please follow me. You are in very good company, sir."

He led me to a room containing a large and long contraption. Small tanks of water made up a lower level, and some had balls of silk bobbing around in them. Higher up was a series of spindles and runners. It looked like something from a Victorian workhouse.

"Silk moths lay their eggs and they hatch into caterpillar, not worm," said the scientist. He turned around and produced a small plate from somewhere. On it were some dead caterpillars. They were small, thin and almost white. "We feed the caterpillars leaves and after maybe five weeks, they make cocoons. It takes three day for the caterpillar to spin their cocoons. By this time, there is one mile of silk thread."

While I cooed in appreciation of this fact, he replaced the caterpillars and picked up another dish. This one contained six white cocoons. I stared at the balls of silk. They resembled fluffy quail eggs. I picked one up and pressed it. It felt suitably silk-like and soft and so I nodded my head in approval. Feeling the need to raise a question, I asked what happened to the larvae inside the cocoons.

"We kill them," the mad scientist said. "Usually we boil them to death or sometimes we pierce them with needles."

"Oh, right."

He pointed at the small tanks of water. "These cocoons are in boiling water." He carefully fished one out. After breaking it apart, he showed me the deceased insect inside. It looked brown and very dead and I actually felt sorry for the tiny creature that had diligently worked so hard to build itself a protective home so it could go through the magical process of metamorphosis. Still, the silk it had produced looked nice.

And with the science portion of my visit over, it was time for the hard sell. The scientist handed me over to a salesman who showed me around a selection of fine silk goods, none with prices on them. He seemed to sense I was not going to be a 'bonanza' customer and rushed through his talk, mainly inviting me to think about how long it took to make a single item, and pointing out how intricate the work was, but then he left me alone. After a minute of pretend looking, I found Susan.

11

"Is it true that women in China can only have one child?" I asked. We were back on the road, with about forty minutes to go before we stopped for lunch.

"Not really," Susan answered from the front seat. "The one-child rule was only ever enforced in cities. In the farms and countryside, people could have two children if a girl was born first. This is what happened to my father and mother. My sister was born first and so my parents asked for permission to have another baby. They hoped for a boy. Then I was born."

"Were your parents annoyed at now having two daughters?"

"Yes, of course. They wanted son. But they accepted things and they loved us entirely. Then we moved to the city where we grew up. Both my sister and I had excellent childhoods. But if my parents had been very rich, they could have tried for third and fourth child. Rich Chinese people could always have more than two children. But all that is changing. Most people can have two children now."

I asked why the one-child policy had changed.

"Because in China there is a lack of girls. I think there are thirty million more men in China than women. It is very serious for my country. Millions of boys will grow up and never find a wife. They will be unhappy about this."

"But it's okay for the girls…"

"Yes. Girls can pick and choose."

As the metropolis of Beijing fell behind us, forests of wispy and bare-branched trees filled both sides of the road. Ahead of us, somewhere, was one of mankind's greatest architectural triumphs and, as we drove closer, Susan told me she had visited it over a hundred times.

"So you must be a little bored by it?"

"Yes, a little."

I asked her whether she had been to any other country outside of China.

"I once went to Hong Kong as a child. I would love to go back."

"Why don't you?" I inquired.

She laughed. "I need to save up lots of money if I want to go Hong Kong. But one day I will go there with my sister. We will shop and shop and shop! All day, all night."

I smiled. She was just like any other young woman, then.

12

After almost an hour's drive, and some seventy kilometres from Beijing, we began to approach Mutianyu, one of the best-preserved sections of the Great Wall. At intervals, foothills, cold and bleak, poked above the tree line, but, so far, the wall was keeping itself hidden.

First, we had to stop for lunch. Inside a large restaurant catering for tourists, a table was set for three people: me, Susan and Zhu, the driver.

"Is okay for us to join you?" asked Susan. Zhu was standing sheepishly behind her, smoking a cigarette. Most Chinese men of a certain age smoked, I'd discovered, and many of them did it indoors. Of course it was, I told her. Susan smiled, turned and said something to Zhu who flashed me a grateful grin, and then shuffled forwards, bowing as he went past me.

Susan went off to talk to the restaurant staff, leaving Zhu and me to sit in uncomfortable silence opposite each other, the language barrier too much of a hurdle to overcome. I grinned and nodded my head, gesturing around the large room as if to say, nice place. Zhu nodded and fiddled with his chopsticks. I picked mine up, tried to manipulate them into a pincer motion. Zhu smiled at my effort and lit another cigarette. I then looked out of the window and caught my first glimpse of the Great Wall. It was too far away to make out properly, but my eyes followed its grey length as it followed a wavy contour of some distant hills.

Susan returned with some metal dishes, clanging them down on the table. A waitress was behind her with even more. Soon dishes filled the empty space between Zhu, Susan and me. "Please help yourself, Mr Jason," Susan said.

For a dreadful moment, I thought all the dishes were for me, and that Susan and Zhu were going to sit and watch me eat. But as soon as I stuck my chopsticks into the rice, they both dived in, grabbing fried dumplings, ginger chicken, shrimp tails, slithers of duck, stir-fried vegetables, flimsy noodles and rice. It was a free-for-all, and delicious to boot. Without doubt, it was the tastiest Chinese food I'd ever had.

The only problem was the chopsticks. My usual lightning speed of food consumption had slowed to such an extent that Susan thought there was something wrong with the food. I explained about my ineptitude with chopsticks and she immediately looked mortified. "I am so sorry, Mr Jason. I did not think..." Before I had chance to stop her, she was out of her seat, rushing over to a waitress. Twenty seconds later, a knife and fork appeared, and I attacked the food with renewed gusto.

It was only later that I realised how much of a buffoon I was. Meal times for most Chinese people involved sitting around an open banquet, dipping into food with chopsticks, as arms crisscrossed and chatter filled the air. And the key part of this mealtime ritual was the humble chopstick. The only part of the stick that touches the mouth is one that will never touch the food. In this way, others can share one dish, hygienically. But then I'd gone and spoilt everything by dipping my fork into everything.

13

The easiest way to get up to the main section of wall at Mutianyu was by cable car. The hardest way was to walk up four thousand steps. Mercifully, there was not enough time to do that and so Susan and I went to the lifts. Instead of being enclosed cable cars, as I'd hoped, the cable car system was more akin to a ski resort chairlift. A two-person seat attached to a large hook was all it was, without even the protection of a safety barrier.

"Come, Mr Jason," instructed Susan, stepping forward into a space that would soon be occupied by the lift. "Be ready to sit down quickly."

Before I had a chance to think about my fear of heights, I followed her into position, waiting for the seat to arrive from behind.

When it did, we both sat down, Susan laughing with delight at how we had dallied with death. But then I realised that getting on the chairlift was the easy part: the ride itself was more fraught with danger. As we lurched into the air, leaving the mountain treetops behind in an instant, I realised that the only thing stopping me from slipping to my doom was the friction of my trousers and my arm gripping the handrail. Susan was not afraid at all, and was even swinging her legs, causing a terrifying extra piece of momentum to our upwards motion.

"I love this part of Great Wall tour," she said, looking down at the tiny trees below us.

I nodded and smiled, though to Susan, it probably looked like a grimace: the grimace of a man about to die. But someone else was suffering worse. Coming down in the opposite direction was a middle-aged Western woman. She was by herself and screaming. Whether she'd pushed her companion out or simply was a sadist, I had no idea, but her shrieking and sobbing actually made me feel better. At least I wasn't *that* bad.

As well as being terrifying, the ascent was absolutely freezing. Snow patches covered the forest floor beneath my feet, and tiny specks floated around us. My exposed hand gripping the handrail was almost numb with cold. "Look, Mr Jason," announced Susan. I stared to where she was pointing. It was some sort of narrow metal track snaking its way down the mountain. "That is the toboggan run," she explained. "We go down it after we finish."

My heart took a dangerous lurch. But then I calmed when I realised that the toboggan would be easier than the cable car. And then we were approaching the uppermost stop. With only a moment to prepare myself, I waited for the seat to hover over the stopping point and jumped off, making a split-second dash to the side to avoid being hit by the seat behind. That done, I stepped onto the Great Wall of China.

Susan went into guide mode again. For the next hour, she took me up and down sections of the wall, pointed out how old it was (about 450 years old), explained the purpose of the watchtowers (to allow soldiers to watch for Mongol invaders), described the height of the walls (about 25 feet) and told me about materials from which the walls were constructed (mostly granite).

The Great Wall looked exactly how it did in photos: stout watchtowers, long stretches of turreted beige wall, and then an expanse of trees tumbling out across high hills. I was surprised at the lack of people, though. Susan explained this was due to the cold and the fact is was a weekday. Come the weekend, she said, it would be packed.

We climbed to a vantage point where I could see the wall stretching from one mountain to the next. I always knew the thing was long, but to see it with my own eyes was something else. Almost unbelievably, the whole thing stretched for almost 4000 miles, longer than the distance between London and New York. If I were in an aeroplane, it would take eight hours to fly from one end to the other.

"You are lucky with weather today," said Susan, bringing me out of my thoughts. "Yesterday was rain and mist. We didn't see much. We can take many good photos. Stand here so I can get the watchtower in background." Once more, I conjured a smile and stood like a lemon while people watched and waited for me to finish.

Snow on the line had temporarily closed the toboggan ride. A bald man wearing a long jacket was guarding the entrance. He looked like Ming the Merciless. When Susan inquired about how long we would have to wait, the man in the jacket shrugged. "It is in the hands of the gods. But if you go down now, the brakes will not work and you will die."

While we milled about, shivering and making small talk, Ming's walkie-talkie crackled into life. After listening for a moment, he turned to us. "We are sending someone down to test the slide. If he survives, then you can go in about five minutes. If he dies, we will bury his bones next to his favourite toboggan."

I asked Susan whether anyone had ever died on the Great Wall.

"Oh yes, many people. Last year a tourist bumped into a Chinese woman and knocked her down some steps. She died at the bottom. Before that, another Chinese woman fainted and fell. That one was really bad."

"So she fell over the side of the Wall?"

"No. She fell on the path. But she fell with her face down and no one turned her over. The wall was very busy that day; many people were taking photos and looking over the side. They saw her fall down but no one went to help. When someone did, it was too late; she was dead: suffocated."

Jesus, what a horrible story.

Ming told us the toboggans were now open for business, and so I climbed aboard my single seat craft, getting a feeling for how the contraption worked. Basically, I had to lean left to go left, lean right to go right. If I pulled on the stick, I would slow down. Susan climbed into the toboggan in front and turned around. "If you see a man waving a flag, slow down. They are the slide marshals."

And then we were off. Susan, being only twenty-five, was zooming off into the distance. I was more cautious, at least at first, and when I rounded the first bend and spotted a marshal, I was surprised to see him urging me to go faster. I realised that I was probably holding up someone behind me. I released a little more brake and then a little more and soon I was zipping down at top speed, turning my body into the turns with glee and dexterity. At the next major bend, a marshal urged me to slow down. I did so, exhilarated and a tiny bit scared. But I got down to the bottom, where Susan was waiting. "Good fun, yeah?"

"Definitely." And I meant it.

It was time for the long drive back to Beijing.

15

That evening I sought out McDonald's. I had no wish to repeat my Hotter than Hell experience of the previous night. As I ate my burger, surrounded by Chinese teenagers jabbering away, I checked my emails and flight bookings for the next few days. Once upon a time, I was going to fly straight home from Beijing, but, due to an airline schedule change a few months back, things had changed considerably. With my refund, I had booked a ridiculous route back to Qatar that involved a stopover in Hong Kong, Singapore and, most excitingly of all, the Maldives.

I was really looking forward to the Maldives. It was a country I'd never been to before. But unlike the vast majority of tourists who visit the Indian Ocean paradise, I was not staying in an outrageously expensive island resort hotel; I was staying in a modestly expensive one called the Hulhule Island Hotel. It was close to the capital Malé (pronounced Marl-ay), a city that most tourists never saw, but one I intended visiting.

The Hulhule had sent me an email confirming my single-night stay. I grimaced at the price. $287 meant it was the most expensive hotel I had ever stayed in. Still, it was cheaper than the Sheraton Full Moon Resort, which wanted almost double, which, in turn, was a snip compared to the Soneva Fushi, a private island resort. According to one website, the Soneva Fushi wanted the utterly ridiculous price of $17000 for one night in its beach villa. Even the cheapest room was over two thousand dollars. So all in all, I thought I had got off lightly with $287. All I had to do was spend the night in Hong Kong and Singapore first. I finished my burger, excited by this prospect.

Clockwise from top left: One of the forced poses Susan insisted I do on the Great Wall of China; Braised Sheep Entrails are just some of the delights on the Menu from Lucifer's Kitchen; Another of Susan's photos, this time in front of Chairman Mao; Inside the Forbidden City; A young soldier standing to attention in Tiananmen Square

Chapter 15: Maldives: a broken paradise

After a night in Hong Kong, staying at the agreeably named Panda Hotel, I flew to Singapore. Six months previously, I'd been there with my wife, enjoying an overpriced Singapore Sling in Raffles, but this time, it was just a fleeting visit: a panorama of tall glitz seen from the window of a taxi.

My hotel had one very special feature, though: a free minibar. Even the alcohol was free. Had I been staying another night, a maid would have replenished the stock. As it stood, I drank one can of gratis Tiger Beer and then put the other in my suitcase. Smuggling alcohol into the Maldives was forbidden, but I reckoned one little can might escape the net. If it didn't, then I'd claim ignorance and say it had been in my suitcase for a few days and I'd forgotten all about it. I went to sleep, tired after rushing around airports for the last couple of days.

The next morning I was back at Changi Airport with the sunrise. Bleary eyed, I navigated my way through security and immigration and found the gate for the flight to Malé. Unsurprisingly, I seemed to be the only solo passenger. Everyone else looked like they were going on their honeymoon. The flight left dead on time, and four hours later, the first atolls started appearing beneath the wing: dazzlingly gorgeous bracelets of turquoise and aquamarine ringed in delicious white. As we approached the airport, the resort islands, circular palm-fringed slices of brochure paradise, came into view. And then they were gone, replaced by a black strip of asphalt. I had arrived in the final country of my travels.

2

Here are some fascinating facts about the Maldives. It is the smallest country in Asia. I know that is not particularly fascinating, so how about this: the Maldives in the smallest *Muslim* country in the world. And what about these facts: the Maldives is 99% ocean and is the lowest country on the planet, with an average height above sea level of only 1.5 metres. Even compared to the Netherlands, a nation famous for its flatness, it is low-lying. The Netherlands would tower over the Maldives by a factor of twenty.

These facts, and a few other less interesting ones, I read in my Lonely Planet guide to the Maldives, which helped pass the time in the queue for immigration. When I reached the front, the uniformed officer wanted to know why I was only staying in the Maldives for one night.

"Just a quick holiday," I offered.

The thin man studied me. Then he shook his head. "Tourists do not come to the Maldives for one night. They come for one week, ten days, maybe even two weeks. One day does not seem right to me." He stared at me, as if assessing me as a drug smuggler or international spy.

"Look," I said, "I'm on my way to Qatar and this was a nice stopover. The other option was Sri Lanka but I thought the Maldives would be nicer."

The immigration officer looked unconvinced but decided to accept me at face value. With a quick stamp in my passport, he welcomed me to the Maldives. Now all I had to do was smuggle in my contraband can of Tiger Beer.

My luggage escaped security without anyone checking, scanning or opening it. I was a smuggler of the highest order, and had saved myself about five dollars by doing so. Alcohol was prohibitively expensive in the Maldives, and often hard to come by. The capital, Malé, didn't sell any at all. When I got to the Hulhule, I would hide the can in the fridge.

Through the other side of the airport, I found myself in an open air building that served as a gathering point for arriving holidaymakers. All the big hotels had representatives, waiting to take their charges straight to paradise: some by speedboat, most by seaplane. A representative of my hotel was waiting, too, even though

I could have walked to the hotel in less than five minutes. It was just around the corner.

"Welcome to the Maldives, Mr Smart," the man in the Hulhule T-shirt beamed. "Please let me take your luggage." I followed him outside and gasped. In front of me was the nicest portion of water I'd ever seen. It looked so lovely that I had to stop there and then to take a photo. The blue water shimmered – actually shimmered – before my eyes, and even the presence of an abandoned luggage trolley along the water's edge could not spoil the view. A few boats bobbed around in front of some palm trees. It really was *paradise*. And this was just the start!

"It's good, isn't it?" said the hotel man. "The water's a great temperature, too. If you have time, you should go snorkelling."

A pilot walked by. He was wearing a white shirt with three gold bars across the shoulders. Instead of trousers and smart shoes, he was wearing black shorts and flip-flops. He probably worked for one of the seaplane companies.

I was the only passenger aboard the hotel's minibus. We drove by the water and I couldn't stop gazing out of the window. If this was how stunningly beautiful the airport looked, imagine what the rest of it was like. And then we arrived at the hotel. It was just across from the runway. When they upgraded me to a deluxe, ocean-view room, I breathed deeply, happy with my choice of the Maldives to end my mammoth trip around Africa and Asia.

3

My room was amazing, and I basked in the view from my upper-storey balcony. The ocean, the tropical greenery and the choice selection of verdant islands lying in the distance: I could not recall a view as good. I took a photo and sent it to my wife. Her response was one word: *Jealous!*

Over to my left was the main island of Malé, the tiny capital of the Maldives. Even though it measured only 2.2 square miles, buildings filled almost every inch of it, cramming in about 150,000 people, making it the fifth most densely populated island in the world, more heavily populated than Manhattan.

I decided to get some lunch in the hotel restaurant, finding myself the only customer. The waiter was a young man from Bangladesh with the improbable name of Shithil. It was even worse than the name of a Filipino man we knew in Qatar. He worked at a frozen yoghurt parlour in one of the shopping malls, and over time, as we became familiar to him, he would give us extra dollops when his boss wasn't looking. The man's name was Venison, as proudly displayed on his nametag. We never questioned this, but secretly pondered plausible reasons for his unlikely moniker. My wife came up with the most likely scenario: many Filipino families named their newborns after what they believed were English-sounding words. Names such as Babe, Angel, Pinky, Pretty and Dear were common. It was this last name that gave my wife the clue she needed. Perhaps the man's parents had wanted to call him something like 'Dear', but because it was a common name, they had perhaps looked in a thesaurus. Unfortunately, they had misspelled dear and so instead of choosing a name such as Charming or Precious, they had gone for the meatier-sounding Venison. Both my wife and I could not think of a more conceivable reason.

Anyway, Shithil told me that a third of the Maldives' population were immigrant workers, mainly from Sri Lanka, India and Bangladesh. "Most work in hotels as waiters. Some work in construction."

I asked whether it was nice to work in the Maldives; after all, most Westerners would give an arm and a leg to work in such blissful surroundings.

"This hotel is okay. Many are not. But not everything is okay in the Maldives, especially over in Malé. They have riots and, sometimes, even murders. Last year, a Bangladeshi waiter was stabbed to death in a cafe."

"Stabbed? Why?"

"I think young Maldivians do not like us. There is much unemployment in the city, and maybe they think we are taking their jobs. There is also a drug problem among the young people. Many are addicted to brown sugar."

And I thought the Maldives was a tranquil retreat of clear water, palm trees and white sand. But it appeared that beneath the veneer, there was a disenfranchised, drug-addicted youth. People often said there was trouble in paradise. Maybe the Maldives was it.

4

My hotel offered a free ferry service to the capital, of which I wanted to avail myself. A helpful man behind the reception desk told me it was not leaving for another half an hour, and that maybe I should sit in the air-conditioned lobby for a while.

While I waited, an airline crew arrived: two male pilots and six or seven female cabin crew. After checking in, they dispersed, carting their small-wheeled luggage towards their rooms. The captain reappeared first, dressed in shorts, sandals and a colourful holiday shirt. He sat just along from me and started checking something on his phone. A couple of female cabin crew appeared next, kitted out in gym gear. After waving at the captain, they disappeared along a corridor.

When the captain glanced in my direction, I smiled and said hello. He nodded back, but before he could return to his emails, or whatever he was doing, I asked him which airline he flew for.

"Emirates. We're based in Dubai. Bad delay this morning. We arrived three hours late." His accent sounded Australian.

"But at least you're in the Maldives."

The captain smiled. "Yeah, the Maldives is one of the better stops. Mind you, a few weeks ago I was in Nairobi. The hotel was nice but the city's a pigsty. Same with Cairo and Bangalore."

I told him I'd been in Nairobi a few weeks ago, and then mentioned some of the other places I'd been.

"I hope you're collecting air miles. You've probably flown more than me."

I glanced at my watch and saw it was time to find the ferry. I said goodbye to the pilot and headed into the heat where I found the small passenger boat sloshing away behind some tennis courts and the swimming pool. At 2.15pm, the boat's engine rumbled to life and a skinny man helped me across from the jetty, even though I was perfectly capable of taking the few steps myself. I sat down on one of the wooden seats, the only passenger. By sticking my head out of the open-air window, I could gaze down into the sea. I snooped on an angelfish and then a sleek silver thing darting around underneath it. In an instant, they were gone.

As we slowly manoeuvred away from the jetty, I watched a seaplane taking off, rising in the warm air, whisking some rich tourists to their private resort. Five minutes later, I had what I thought might be the best view of Malé. A panorama of high-rise and modern buildings nestled around a gigantic red and green Maldivian flag. To the flag's right was a striking gold dome belonging to a mosque. It sparkled like a bauble in the sun. Scattered around everything was lush tropical vegetation. Malé might not be as nice as the private atolls, but it still had oodles of tropical charm. And as we passed between the harbour walls, the ocean suddenly became calm. I noted that the journey had taken just twelve minutes.

5

A line of jetties lay inside Malé Harbour. As we pulled up alongside some small ferries, I noticed a fishing boat next to us. The vessel was called Bigfish-7. On deck, an Indian-looking man was tending to a net, possibly checking for loose threads. Above him, some washing was drying in the sun.

I disembarked and took in the lie of the land. Up close, Malé looked chaotic and grimy. The shiny office blocks now looked crowded and dirty. To my right was a parking space for small motorbikes and scooters. It was crammed to capacity. Behind them was a cluster of shops and market stalls; in front of one was a row of upturned tuna fish. Everywhere around was noisy with beeps, shouting and outboard motors.

I walked forward towards the massive flag. It stood in a small area known as Republic Square, a well-tended rectangle of flowerbeds and grass. The police headquarters, a large blue and white building, took up one side of the square. A uniformed man came out and then disappeared around a corner. Two more police officers came out with riot shields. They chatted for a while, then headed away from the harbour. I decided to do the same thing.

I had three missions to complete in Malé. One was to find the Beehive Hotel. I'd read that the Beehive had a rooftop café that offered the best views of the city. After that, I wanted to see the public beach, the closest I would get to a topical retreat on the whole island, and, finally, I intended to visit the Tsunami Monument.

I turned right from the harbour and walked past the motley collection of convenience stores, fresh fish stalls and fruit-and-vegetable sellers. Their customers were mostly men, with only a few hijab-wearing women browsing among them. I stepped into an expansive market filled with yams, coconuts, watermelons, papayas and huge bunches of dangling bananas. Feeling peckish, I bought a banana from one leather-skinned, toothy old man. When I passed him a dollar, he handed me a handful of local currency, the exotic sounding *rufiyaa*, as my change. Outside, I was walking along Boduthakurufannu Magu, a thin street that ran around the northern edge of the island. Home to dingy shops, its edges formed parking spaces for motorbikes and delivery vans. Around and between them stood dark-skinned men conversing in a foreign tongue. Anyone magically transported here, and made to guess their location, would probably say somewhere in India or Sri Lanka, which was not surprising since immigrants from those countries started settling on the islands and atolls almost two centuries previously. Malé Island was as far from most people's idea of what the Maldives looked like as a jumbo jet was from a car.

On my right was the ocean, a view blocked by more fishing boats and a large and long grey building called the Maldives Ports Limited. On my left were ugly tower blocks. The smell of rotting fruit was coming from somewhere, and I found the source of it: an overfilled metal rubbish bin. I stepped over the mess, passed a few hardware shops, and finally reached the western edge of the island.

6

The western part of Malé had a much better view of the ocean. Beyond the Japanese-built sea wall, a few cargo ships were ponderously making their way into open sea. Behind them was the island of Villingili, and behind that was another island that belched smoke continuously. Its name was Thilafishi, or Rubbish Island.

Every day, the Maldives produces hundreds of tons of rubbish. Some of it comes from holidaymakers, but most of it is from the capital. And all this rubbish has to go somewhere; since Malé Island cannot cope with any, a steady stream of ships transports tons of garbage to Thilafishi Island. When they dump it, teams of Bangladeshi workers toil over the rotting and smelling mess. Rising above their heads is a constant cloud of acrid, toxic smoke. Up close, the island is a large rubbish dump, with litter and waste covering it from end to end. A few years ago, when rubbish started spilling into the ocean, the Maldivian government put a temporary ban on the gigantic rubbish bin, but the ban didn't last long and soon the boats started delivering again. Day and night, summer and winter, Rubbish Island burns the detritus of paradise. I wondered whether any visiting tourists even knew of its existence.

Before seeking out the Beehive Hotel and ticking off my number one thing to do, I ambled along the western coast, passing the Indira Gandhi Memorial Hospital (a large white building with a fetching orange roof), walking as far as the ferry port, where a flotilla of small boats waited to transport passengers to and from Villingili Island. Nearby was the cafe where a group of men murdered the young Bangladeshi waiter.

On 22nd March 2015, four masked raiders stormed into the Lhiyanu Café and attacked a 24 year old cafe worker called Shaheen Mia. After stabbing him in the neck and chest, the gang fled on motorbikes. No suspects have ever been arrested. A few days later, another young immigrant worker was found strangled in his small apartment. And just a month before my visit to the Maldives, a local shop owner was found dead in a yam field on Malé Island. Before murdering him, his assailants had robbed the man. With unemployment and drug taking seemingly rampant among the disaffected local youth of the Maldives, it seemed things were coming to a head.

I noticed a few gaunt-looking young men with scraggly beards and long hair, but all of them were just getting on with their day like everyone else. None gave me any hard stares or bothered me for money. In fact, I felt perfectly safe, and so I retraced my steps until I came to the start of Majeedhee Magu Road, the island's main road. It ran through the centre of the island, bisecting Malé. Instead of being a multi-laned highway, the capital's most important road was just a thin street.

Majeedhee Magu Road could not cope with the volume of traffic, pedestrians and buildings spilling out across its edges. Motor scooters and cars had to weave along its length, avoiding the people walking in the road, the bikes parked in it and the building materials haphazardly left in piles. A quarter of the way along its length, I stopped to take stock, consulting my pathetically poor Lonely Planet map. As I did so, a young man approached. He looked like any of the young men I'd come across, except instead of ignoring me, he wanted to help. And he *genuinely* wanted to help. I told him about the Beehive Hotel.

"I think I know," he told me, scanning the buildings nearby. "But it is not along this street. You need to go along one of the side streets."

I thanked the man but ignored his advice. My map told me the hotel *was* along the main road, and so I carried on walking. A few minutes later, another young man on a motorbike stopped and asked whether I needed assistance. He told me that the hotel was behind me somewhere.

"So it's not along this road?"

"I do not think so." He then offered to give me a lift on the back of his bike. I was tempted, but I thanked him and declined. As he drove off, I thought about how friendly the locals were. Instead of trying to murder me, they wanted to help.

I passed a gaggle of schoolgirls, all attired in white hijabs and tiny green ties. None paid me any attention and, as I passed a large building site, I realised I had no idea where the Beehive Hotel was. While I looked this way and that, wondering whether to go forwards or backwards, left or right, a third man stopped to aid me. He ended up being the best help because he walked me right to the entrance of the hotel. The other men had been correct; the Beehive was not on the main road because it had moved. As well as this inconvenience, it had done away with its rooftop cafe.

7

I heard the dull thud first, closely followed by the sight of a stricken pigeon. It had flown into the path of an oncoming taxi and was now lying on the pavement by my foot. It was still alive, but badly injured. I wanted to do something, but couldn't. It would never fly again, that much was clear. I should put the poor thing out of its misery, but knew I could not do such a thing. As it tried to flutter its broken wings, I felt suddenly and overwhelmingly sad: the sight of its eyes, and the opening and closing beak was too much to bear. It knew it was going to die, and my only hope was that it would be quick. Mercifully, it was, and just a few moments later, it lay still, an invisible casualty of the road. I found a discarded piece of cardboard and moved the pigeon to the edge of the path, close to an old wall. At least in death it would be safe from trampling feet.

Ten minutes later, still walking Majeedhee Magu Road, passing small shopping centres, tour group offices and flyers for Maldivian business schools, I couldn't shake off the image of the pigeon. It was silly really; after all, it was just a pigeon, and they got knocked down, captured by cats and squashed by tyres every day. I tried to conjure the view from my hotel room, which managed to cheer me slightly. The sight in front of me buoyed me further: a tiny slice of tropical niceness called the Artificial Beach.

The beach was a dainty D-shaped sliver of white sand and palm trees bordered by a stunningly blue reach of ocean. It was the only place on the island where the locals could enjoy what rich tourists had elsewhere else. There was a sign telling me that wearing a bikini was not allowed, which was a shame. Taking advantage of the sea were four women, all covered from head to toe in black burkas. They were splashing, laughing and bobbing around with wanton abandon. Nearby was a beach cafe. I sat under its shade and ordered a Diet Coke. While I waited for it, I noticed a man take a seat at the far side of the beach. His chosen spot was a shaded area under a straw parasol. The man looked homeless, in possession of some wild black hair and an unkempt frizzy beard. He wasn't homeless, though, at least I didn't think so, for he had a plastic box with some sandwiches in them. He seemed to be waiting for someone, and that someone turned out to be a something: a cat. An equally unkempt tabby jumped up and sat on his lap. The man stroked it affectionately and then handed the cat something from his box.

My drink came and, because I was now in such a good mood, I ordered a sandwich myself. By the time it came, the frizzy-haired man was standing up. The cat remained on the bench. After waving goodbye to the animal, he picked up a red surfboard and headed away from the beach. As for me, I pored over the map. The Tsunami Monument was not far and was my next port of call.

8

On the morning of 26 December 2004, one of the world's worst natural disasters was about to unfold. Originating under the sea near Java, Indonesia, a monumental earthquake was gearing up to unleash a tidal wave of Biblical proportions. When it did, thunderous waves raced across the Indian Ocean in all directions just as the Maldives was waking up.

At around 9.30am on that fateful day, without any warning whatsoever, the tsunami reached the islands. Instead of a towering wall of water, it seemed as if the land was sinking. Within a few minutes, four feet of water had submerged almost every piece of Maldivian land. But this was not gentle water that sloshed around people's feet and flooded their home; no, it was the rapid advance of tidal water. Ships were tipped over, boats were lifted and deposited inland. Water sluiced through the shops and marketplaces of downtown Malé. Cars, motorbikes and people were swept away. Fish were seen swimming along the streets. One man managed to cling to a coconut tree while the swirling torrent systematically destroyed the island's infrastructure beneath him.

Almost immediately, the nation's power failed, rendering telephones, the airport and harbours redundant. The force of water ripped houses down, leaving thousands instantly homeless. On one of the resort islands, the waves were strong enough to wash away beach homes. Five minutes after the flood, the water retreated, leaving the islanders to survey the damage. The tsunami had caused over a billion dollars' worth of destruction. If not for the outlying coral reefs, the damage would have been greater. As it was, 82 people lost their lives, including two Brits. One was a 60 year old woman from Southampton who had been standing in the doorway of her beach bungalow when the wave hit. The force of the water sent her and the bungalow out to sea. The other casualty was a 37-year-old who happened to be snorkelling with his wife at the time of the tragedy. She somehow survived.

The Maldivian authorities built a monument to the 82 people who died, placing it on the south-eastern tip of the island, in a quiet area away from the bustle of downtown. It sits on a little platform at the water's edge and consists of 82 individual steel rods, arranged in a ring, each engraved with a name. Encircling the tubular structure are twenty silver spheres, each one representing a Maldivian atoll.

I was the only person there, and spent a few minutes of contemplation, thinking of the people who had lost their lives on the Maldives that day.

9

Back in central Malé, I came across a dainty white lighthouse. It was sitting by the side of a road, well away from the sea. It was an unusual location for a lighthouse, I thought, certainly not tall enough for ships to see it, but then I realised it was actually the minaret of the nearby Friday Mosque, the city's oldest place of worship, dating from the seventeenth century. The mosque wasn't as nice as the minaret, looking like a house with a tin roof, and so I went off to investigate the golden dome peeking between some buildings.

It turned out to belong to the similarly-named Grand Friday Mosque. This one was more like it because it looked spanking new. It was massive and white, dripping with grey zigzags and dazzling golds. I was about to have a wander around its grounds when I heard a commotion.

It sounded like someone hollering through a loudspeaker. I headed towards the ferry jetties, close to the flagpole. Once there, I could see the source of the noise: a man with a loudspeaker walking around Republic Square. With him were other men holding placards, none of which I could read. A small crowd had gathered to watch, and traffic had slowed to a standstill. Underneath the police headquarters, a line of policemen with riot shields and batons stood watching, too. I was reassured to see they didn't seem particularly alarmed. After the protestors marched up and down for a bit, shouting and causing a scene, they trudged off down the street, with a few riot officers following them. As the crowd under the flag dispersed, I walked to a shop to buy some snorkelling equipment.

"What was all that about?" I asked the shopkeeper, a professorial gent with a slight stoop.

"You mean the noise and shouting, sir?"

I nodded.

"It was government protestors. They do this all the time. Sometimes, they shout and screech late at night and then protests turn violent. I am in fear of my shop when this happens."

I grabbed my snorkel and made my way back to the Hulhule Hotel ferry jetty. I had earmarked the rest of the afternoon for swimming and lazing by the hotel's beach.

10

The next morning, with a few hours to kill before my flight back to Qatar, I was sitting aboard the ferry, heading back to Malé Island. Republic Square was as I left it – peaceful but busy; the flag was still rippling and the sun was shining down over it all. Over to my right, a man was wheeling a barrow of large fish. The banana sellers had a fresh batch, and all over the islands, the Maldives was preparing itself for another day. As for me, I headed past the golden-domed mosque, negotiating my way through the narrow and overcrowded streets of Malé. My destination was over in the West: the Villingili Ferry Terminal.

Almost there, I came across a driving school. A few cars were manoeuvring slowly around a rectangle of land, reversing into spaces and driving up small ramps to simulate going over hills. A man was riding a motorbike in a tight circle. He had an L-plate on his back. I watched them awhile, wondering whether they were ever allowed to practise on the real streets surrounding the school. Probably not, I wagered.

Villingili Ferry Terminal was a light-blue holding pen for passengers. I bought a ticket for the equivalent of 15p, and boarded the long wooden ferry by way of some metal steps at the rear. Since every seat was already taken, I took up station at the back with all the other late boarders. The crossing was nothing special, apart from the view and, ten minutes after leaving Malé Island, the ferry pulled up at Villingili Island and we all climbed out.

The island was tiny and I intended to walk around its circumference. While my fellow passengers dispersed, the first thing that struck me was the lack of traffic. Indeed, the only cars were a few taxis, which were the only vehicles allowed.

I walked north, passing gorgeous beaches devoid of people. In the distance was Malé, a metropolis compared to where I was. I reached a small fishing harbour, noticing a man fast asleep in a hammock. He was not alone. Dotted all over the island of Villingili were men in hammocks. While they slumbered, the women of the island were scrubbing steps, hanging washing out, flapping rugs to free them from dust, and nursing infants. I nodded to myself: I could live on Villingili.

I found a gorgeous beach on the northwest of the island: a sweep of white sand, edged by tropical palms, lapped by a soothing Indian Ocean. It was a page from a travel brochure. Except for one small detail: out at sea was Rubbish Island, its fires still burning.

Walking further, I found myself well away from any homes and boats; instead, I was following a thin trail that led between some trees. Above me, hidden somewhere, was a bird making a throaty call, its song rising dramatically in pitch towards the end. The trail delivered me onto another beach, this one not as nice as the others I'd seen in the Maldives. Rubbish was the reason: debris from Rubbish Island, I thought.

I ventured around the other side of Villingili. From somewhere came the sound of music: a raucous thump of drums, distorted guitars and raspy vocals, precisely the kind of music I would *not* associate with the Maldives. I clambered around some palms, causing spiky-backed lizards to scatter in alarm, until I found the source of the heavy metal. A low-roofed building surrounded by an impenetrable fence had a sign on it: VilliMalé Detox Center. This was where the drug addicts of the Maldives came to be cured, with the aid of thrash metal, by the sounds of it.

My circuit of the island was almost finished, and it was just in time to catch the ferry back to the capital. Forty minutes later, I was back at the Hulhule Hotel packing for the final time.

11

So that was it: the Maldives done and dusted. China and Mongolia visited and ticked. South Korea, Iran, Tunisia, South Africa, Namibia, Madagascar, Mauritius and Djibouti all finished with: eleven countries across two vast continents: a trip of ridiculous and arduous proportions, involving twenty-three flights, fourteen hotels and numerous currencies. A trip of a lifetime.

The highlights? The salt lake in Djibouti stood out, and so did Kish Island, an unexpected delight of the Middle East. Driving to the Demilitarized Zone between both Koreas had made my blood rush, and, despite the cold, I'd enjoyed Ulaanbaatar's fixation with Chinggis Khaan. I'd also discovered that the Great Wall of China was actually worthy of its entrance fee, especially if you get to take a toboggan to the bottom. But I was glad to finish up in the Maldives, where I had discovered some of the realities of the island nation. Not all ocean paradises are as they seem. But the real highlight of the trip was Madagascar. Seeing the lemurs, the chameleons, the vivid landscape and the colourful people who inhabited this most majestic of islands had been the definite highlight.

But I was ready to go back home now. There were only so many hotels and airports I could stand in one prolonged period of time. So with my bags in preparation for my flight back to Doha, Qatar, another trip came to an end.

Clockwise from top left: The Maldives is really this stunningly beautiful; The Tsunami Monument; Evening sets in and the scooters go home; A fisherman waits for his crew; Banana selling in downtown Malé; Approaching the ferry jetties of Malé; Interesting patterns on the Grand Friday Mosque

Message from Jason

Thanks for reading about my travels around Africa and Asia. If you enjoyed it, I would really appreciate a review on Amazon. Just a few lines will do. Small-time authors such as me rely on word of mouth for exposure. Just go to Amazon, type Africa to Asia by Jason Smart and you'll be there.

If you have enjoyed this book by Jason Smart, then perhaps you will also like his other books, which are all available from Amazon.

The Red Quest

Flashpacking through Africa

The Balkan Odyssey

Temples, Tuk-tuks and Fried Fish Lips

Panama City to Rio de Janeiro

Bite Size Travel in North America

Crowds, Colour, Chaos

Rapid Fire Europe

Meeting the Middle East

From Here to Anywhere

Africa to Asia

Take Your Wings and Fly

Visit his website **www.theredquest.com** for more details.

Printed in Great Britain
by Amazon